THE OLYMPIANS

DEDICATED TO THE FELLOWS
OF THE DALLAS INSTITUTE OF HUMANITIES AND CULTURE

THE OLYMPIANS

Ancient Deities as Archetypes

edited by

JOANNE H. STROUD

contributors

GAIL THOMAS   ROBERT SARDELLO   JOANNE H. STROUD
DONALD COWAN   FREDERICK TURNER   LOUISE COWAN
DONA S. GOWER   EILEEN GREGORY   LYLE NOVINSKI
MARY VERNON   DANIEL RUSS   WILLIAM BURFORD

CONTINUUM · NEW YORK

1996

The Continuum Publishing Company
370 Lexington Avenue
New York, NY 10017

Copyright © 1995 by The Dallas Institute Publications

Design and Typography: Janis Lilly

Printed in the United States of America

Library of Congress Cataloging-in-Publication Data

The Olympians : ancient deities as archetypes / edited by Joanne H.
Stroud; contributors, Gail Thomas ... [et al.].
    p.   cm.
Includes biographical references and index.
Originally published: Dallas, Tex. : Dallas Institute
Publications. Dallas Institute of Humanities and Culture, c1995.
    ISBN 0-8264-0898-2 (pbk.)
    1. Gods, Greek. 2. Goddesses, Greek. 3. Mythology, Greek.
I. Stroud, Joanne. II. Thomas, Gail.
    [BL782.O48 1996]
    292.2'11—dc20   96-12688
                                            CIP

Photograph, page 138: with permission of the Dallas Museum of Art

"The Wereman" and "Departure from the Bush" from *The Journals of Susanna Moodie*
by Margaret Atwood. Copyright © Oxford University Press Canada 1970.
An excerpt from "Procedures for Underground" from *Procedures for Underground* by
Margaret Atwood. Copyright © Oxford University Press Canada 1970.
Reprinted by permission of Oxford University Press Canada.

Contents

Editor's Preface

O n your first exposure to Homer in school, you may have been as confused as I was by the interaction of Olympian deities and mortals. Why were some humans favored by the gods, while others aroused their ire? Why did this teeming pantheon of gods and goddesses behave in such unpredictable, capricious, and even human ways? Why, almost three thousand years after Homer described their antics, are they still so alive to us today in a markedly dissimilar age?

At a conference in 1990, twelve Fellows of the Dallas Institute of Humanities and Culture sought answers to these questions. With unanimity, they concluded that the Olympian legacy is still valuable as an image for understanding human motivations, longings, and desires. Viewed through disciplines as dissimilar as literature, physics, art history, and psychology, the consensus was that these presences can serve as mythical mirrors, reflecting the depths and convolutions of being human. Paraphrasing Daniel Noel, they can teach us how to imagine the mythic elements in our own lives.

My personal view, fashioned by many years of study of Jungian psychology, is that the way in which the gods and goddesses employed their superhuman resources, the way in which they drew upon their limitless reserves of élan, or spirit, offer intimations of what is possible for mortals if we strive to understand them. In so many ways, they reveal us to ourselves—the divine, dazzling parts, the troublesome tensions. Their sovereign worlds resonated with squabbles, battles, love, deceits, and threats. Yet, their profound spiritual insights were never obscured, nor their recognition that collective harmony could only be achieved through respect for each other's spheres of authority. In similar fashion, we need to embrace a plurality of perspectives in order to forge identities, with all their paradoxes. In our strengths we find our culpabilities, in our weaknesses our redeeming transformations. Above all, the Greeks teach us toleration.

In his introduction to the *Iliad*, Richard Lattimore offers a revealing vignette that illumines how the deities function on multiple levels of psychological action:

> When Helen protests to Aphrodite, who has dragged her off to Troy for the sake of an unworthy man, ...she is doing two things at once. First, she is appealing to a supernatural person who is making her do what that person wants. Second, she is talking to herself, to that susceptibility (her Aphrodite) which has made her behave in a manner which the excellent mind of Helen considers idiotic. (54)

In James Hillman's view, the classic Greeks excelled because their religion, which they lived on a daily basis, provided them with an incomparable awareness of the dynamics of human behavior. From this grounding emerged an enlightened perception of the soul, one less confined than in some monotheistic faiths. The Greeks felt free to let their imaginations roam. They became aware of eternal psychological patterns, and this enabled them to develop the artistic and philosophical realms—what we call the humanities. Their creative thirst for knowledge also led them beyond the earth-centered world into cosmic studies of astronomy and astrology. The images drawn from their divinely-inspired mythology became an enduring allegorical yardstick by which western cultural history is still being measured.

On the level of psyche, each of us has a Zeus to express our wrath when justice seems offended; each a Hera when the one we love seems to be drawn away from us. We become like Ares when the energy for engagement strikes at our heart, like Apollo when we stand back and take a cool look, like Hermes when we have to resort to trickery to get our wishes. We have our Athena moments when we are able to reason and persuade with conviction, our Artemis interludes when we need to slip away, our Hestia periods when we want to stay at home and keep the nourishing fires burning. Poseidon rules our tempestuous moments, Demeter reminds us of our connection with living things—the earth, our mother, our daughter. Aphrodite is the enhancer of all ephemeral moments of sensual beauty; then, Hephaistos helps us to mold that beauty into a more enduring art form. Frederick Turner expresses this point: "The genius of polytheism, the tragic joy of polytheism is that there is a god for every aspect of reality, however contradictory." Today, even if Hera or Aphrodite are not directly intermingling in our lives, we can acknowledge the pragmatic benefits to be derived from an understanding of the interplay between the Twelve Olympians.

The lovely housing for these papers was provided by a team functioning somewhat like a guild in the Middle Ages—which is often the way the Institute operates with everyone contributing a specialty. In particular, I want to name Marie Basalone, Adrienne Cox, Frank Luckner of our production staff; Cynthia Stibolt and Jane Milburn; and especially Janis Lilly whose artistic patterning of the book makes it so appealing. In all three books of the trilogy, Gail Thomas, Robert Sardello, and I were in constant communication. Finally, our thanks are extended to George Parker Jr., whose Western European Architecture Foundation generously supported this project.

JOANNE H. STROUD
Dallas

October 1995

ZEUS
THE FORM OF THINGS

DONALD COWAN

O ne is invariably tempted in speaking of Zeus to assume his guise in costume. The garb I would choose was used more than fifty years ago in the opening scene of *Amphitryon '38*, the delightful portrayal by Lunt and Fontanne of Zeus' visit to Alcmene, the outcome of which was to be the birth of Herakles. The stage was filled by a large sculptured backdrop of the blue heavens with a white cloud on which reclined Zeus and Hermes, their faces turned toward the audience, their legs stretched upward behind them, with their two short-skirted bare derrières the center of our attention. Dramas nearly always make a contract of sorts with the audience, allowing viewers to know at the beginning what kind of play they are to see. This was to be no tragedy.

The situation that moved the play *Amphitryon* along was of the sort that has always dogged Zeus' reputation. One scene showed Leda commiserating with Alcmene, bringing up that business with the swan that produced Helen and Clytemnestra, and possibly Castor and Pollux as well—though in separate swan-eggs. Turning back through mythology, one recalls that in another such incident, Semele produced Dionysus for Zeus. "Produced" may be the wrong word: when Semele demanded that Zeus appear to her in his full glory, the consequent bolt of lightning reduced her to cinders. According to the fable, Zeus snatched the babe from the ashes and clapped it into his thigh, where it completed its prenatal maturation. The status of Semele's son Dionysus as a god, then, has a bit of ambiguity about it. As a rule, when Zeus couples with a goddess, he generates a god; when he couples with a mortal, he produces a mortal-hero. Obviously Semele, daughter of Cadmus, was a mortal, as her ashes attest.

("Semele," incidentally, is a name for the cthonic, the underworldly.) Apparently Dionysus' second birth from Zeus' thigh qualifies him as a god, a very earthy one, to be sure—wine, ecstasy, disorder, chaos are the fruits of Bacchus and his pards. He is the god of destruction and renewal.

The legends concerning Zeus' amours always have some analogical, allegorical, even anagogical significance that raises them to the level of myth. In this encounter with the young woman who is to be the mother of Dionysus, this fathering god has struck into the underworld to retrieve the presence of chaos necessary for new meaning to be formed. Without something powerful to upset it, the human order would quickly stagnate in its own structures. There had to be a Dionysus in order for Zeus' will to be accomplished; so Zeus himself sees to the engendering of the frenzied god.

Zeus' further paternity produced the nine Muses by the Titaness Mnemosyne—memory—in nine successive nights, as legend has it. The three Graces came by way of Eurynome. Athena is Zeus' daughter by Metis (counsel), Hermes his son by Maia ("midwife," the word Socrates uses to describe his own maiauetic teaching). Aphrodite, according to Homer, is Zeus' child by Dione, although Hesiod's account of the sea goddess rising out of the foam from Uranus' castrated parts makes a more graphic story. Apollo and Artemis are Zeus' progeny by Leto. And there are more: in an unguarded moment, Zeus names for Hera several other amours: the wife of Ixion, who bore him Peirithoos; Europa, mother of Minos; and Demeter, mother of Persephone. Hebe, Hephaistos, and Ares are Hera's offspring, with or without Zeus' help. (Like Gaia, she has a parthenogenetic power.)

A number of tales exist concerning each of Zeus' adventures; to follow even one of them out would lead us far astray. Suffice it to say that Zeus is the father of gods and of men—many gods and many men. But it would be impious of us to leer at the implications. For, as I've begun seeing in later life, Zeus' infidelities have a purpose.

Just as in the Amphitryon play, it was Leda's account of her amours with the swan that awakened my irreverence toward the lustful Zeus, so it may have been Yeats' rendering of that same event that began my redeification of this lord of Mt. Olympos:

> A shudder in the loins engenders there
> The broken wall, the burning roof and tower
> And Agamemnon dead.
> Being so caught up
> So mastered by the brute blood of the air,
> Did she put on his knowledge with his power
> Before the indifferent beak could let her drop?
> ("Leda and the Swan")

Yeats ponders the mystery of this engendering of Helen; the Trojan War, the fall of the great city, the triumph of the Achaians and the murder of their leader on his homecoming to Clytemnestra—in fact, all of Greek civilization—are contained in it. What is implied in the poetic imagination, then, we might say, is that the act itself is not a simple act of lust but a movement toward the fulfillment of history. Did the woman who became the vessel for the divine seed of heroes and heroines have a glimpse of her lover's knowledge in the act of lovemaking? "Before the indifferent beak could let her drop"—in this phrase one is shocked into attention by its reference to divine indifference, the level-eyed gaze of the god.

Zeus' reign represents the coming of intellect to divinity; his triumph over the Titans signifies the end of brute force as paradigm for the cosmos. One of Zeus' exclusive characteristics is *diké*—justice, meaning rightness; right judgment, order, purpose, or, as it is frequently called, his "plan." The term for excellence, *arete*, the main ethical term of praise in Greek (says Arthur Adkins), was originally applicable to competitive qualities—valor and skill. The cooperative virtues of justice and righteousness were *dikaiosyne*. As we see Zeus in his justice, we merge these latter qualities with the term *arete*.

Zeus is the generative principle that sustains history, magnifies it, and gives it form. His father, Kronos, may have started time, but it is Zeus who engenders history, something that has sequence and recountability—that is to say, has meaning. And it is important to point out that, for almost every engendering adventure—though not the one Yeats describes—there is at least one recounting that makes of the encounter an immaculate conception. Some say Dionysus was begotten upon Semele by a potion she drank. Further, according to Aeschylus, Zeus engendered in the lovely cow-maiden Io, by means of a single touch, the dark-skinned Epaphos, one of whose descendants would be Herakles, the unbinder of Prometheus. And yet another incident is found in the hero Perseus, born of Danaë, whose father protected her virginity by locking her in a brazen cage, through whose bars Zeus poured as a shower of gold into her lap. Perseus' son, Electryon, incidentally—if anything in myth is ever incidental—is the father of Alcmene. That gorgeous, virtuous creature is the great-granddaughter of Zeus by way of an already-established hero and is therefore the woman Zeus selects to bear the yet greater hero Herakles. Earlier, Teiresias had prophesied the destruction of Olympia by a monstrous race of giants unless such a hero would rise up to destroy them. Herakles is the necessary champion. So it is always that, as Hermes says of the Amphitryon deception, "Zeus has his reasons."

There is no essential conflict between this last account of Herakles' origin and the prophecy of his advent in the Io-Prometheus story. We can construct a genealogy that runs from Io through Perseus to Alcmene, with Zeus reentering the biological stream every third generation. But generally any search for canonicity in the Greek myths is headed for frustration. There are too many wellsprings in too many lands, cultures, and times ever to merge the various tales, legends, rituals, celebrations, and representations into a coherent account. Caroline Gordon had some such ambition in mind with her penultimate novel *The Glory of Hera*, but it lacks an index that would have made the volume a handy reference; and, too, the novel is not sufficiently documented with arcane source materials to qualify as mythography. Though sadly neglected, her novel is a great demonstration of how *poiesis*—the poetic imagination—makes order out of the chaos that scholarship provides. Robert Graves' two-volume compendium, though handy, undertakes no such unification, nor does the profound scholarly work of Karl Kerényi (*The Religion of the Greeks and Romans*) or the philosophic explorations of Walter Otto (*The Homeric Gods*).

Of course the primary source, for us as it was for the Greeks, is Homer, particularly the *Iliad*, and the secondary source is Hesiod's *Theogony*. All other scholarship on Greek sources is tertiary. But then there is the redaction of the Roman world, with its great work, Virgil's *Aeneid*. Myth grows in all directions; even we ourselves add to it. The true myth resides in one's own mind, comprehensive and amorphous, ready to change its shape, like the old man of the sea, whenever one attempts to grasp it too firmly.

And one must acknowledge the difficulty time presents in myth. Maybe old Kronos should have stayed out of it. Our Olympian gods are immortal and so are many others. But not all gods are deathless. Nymphs—those of fountains, springs, and rivers—generally are not invulnerable, although sea nymphs may be. Those that inhabit trees, dryads or wood nymphs, die with their hosts. One should prune the oak with tenderness, aware of the divinity within. When immortality enters the picture, sequence becomes unique to the tale being told. Mythic time has its own universality, not the time our factual chronicles beat out. Genealogy charts for Zeus' progeny showing frequent looping reentries of Zeus into the different generations remind us that it is not just Oedipus who has this feedback arrangement for his own genes. And one of the great principles of rationality—that an effect cannot be its own cause—just isn't necessarily so, as we surely know, deep within us. We all have some trace of the far-seeingness of Zeus, of fore-knowing the outcome which we ourselves must bring about by yet unknown means. The truths that myths convey have very little to do with argument—understanding, yes: logic, no.

This seeing things from afar spreads a panorama of space before

Zeus that endows an action with completeness, as does the spreading out in time. Zeus looks down from Olympos and sees mankind in its simplest dimensions. We are inclined to think of Olympos as Heaven or Paradise, and in a sense it is; but it is also for the folk imagination and that of the poet a fictional city on an actual mountain in north-east Thessaly, the highest point in Greece. When Zeus views the Trojan War, he must move to Mt. Ida, the highest point near Troy, where "rejoicing in the pride of his strength [he] sat down on the mountain, looking out over the city of Troy and to the ships of the Achaians." Zeus is therefore not getting a space-shot of the earth. He is not so far away that he does not see people in their individuality. From Mt. Ida, he sees both the city of Troy and the ships of the Achaians—both sides of the conflict. He knows when every hero falls and mourns each, one by one.

Zeus-the-intellect is the one to whom earthly events have meaning and beauty. His is the clear intelligence that the Greeks speak of as *nous*. Kerényi declares: "With Zeus, the *Nous* shows itself pure and perfect...it discovers everything without seeking, indeed everything discovers itself to it...the object of *nous* is what really is." Rachel Bespaloff (in her *On the Iliad*) calls him "Zeus the watcher," and attributes to this divine spectator the meaning of the poem. It is Zeus' observation of all, she says, that keeps the Trojan war from being merely a bloody battle. The heroic action, the beautiful deed, the sacrifice—all these take on meaning to the shining eyes of the god who feels not love for his creatures such as Israel's Jahweh feels, but admiration and sometimes friendship.

Passages from the *Iliad* give some sense of Zeus' "watching" of earthly events: not simply observing, but brooding, gazing, assessing, contemplating, knowing. "I think of these men though they are dying," he says to the assembled gods. "Even so, I shall stay here upon the fold of Olympos / sitting still, watching, to pleasure my heart." After his son Sarpedon is killed he will not "turn the glaring of his eyes from the strong encounter / but kept gazing forever upon them, in spirit reflective and pondered hard." And once, when the fight is raging so fiercely below that the other gods draw back in a kind of horror:

> To these gods
> the father gave no attention at all, but withdrawn from them
> and rejoicing in the pride of his strength sat apart from the others,
> looking out over the city of Troy and the ships of the Achaians,
> watching the flash of the bronze, and men killing and men killed.

It is in Zeus' eyes that valorous deeds have an ultimate meaning. As Milton writes of Jove in his pastoral elegy "Lycidas": "As he pronounces justly on each deed / Of so much fame in heaven expect thy meed."

So, who or what is Zeus, the lord of Olympos?

Lloyd-Jones writes, "It is difficult...to know Zeus' nature; is he the necessity of Nature or the mind of man?" It is something of an evasion, I say, to make him either one. But neither is he fortune or fate or some statistical outcome of a random process.

Martin Nilsson writes about Zeus (in *Greek Piety*) : "The levelling out of the total of the different chances which man meets with, so that ill luck counterbalances good luck, could not be ascribed to any particular god but formed part of the divine government of the universe. Hence they spoke of 'the god,' 'the divine,' 'deity' as its origin; ...Zeus might replace this general expression." Perhaps. But neither for Greek or for us is an ineffable presence of probability a very satisfying chief deity. Admittedly, we anthropomorphize him when we call him father, recognizing his generative role, his governing function, his intellectual capacity, his dispensing of justice, his providential concern—all of which somewhat get out of hand, certainly, in the magnitude and complexity of controlling the universe.

It seems better to think of him—as the Greek poets obviously did—as in some sense the god beyond the gods: *theos:* the god. Aeschylus has his chorus in the Agamemnon speak, out of their foreboding of ill for the House of Atreus:

Zeus: whatever he may be, if this name
pleases him in invocation,
thus I call upon him.
I have pondered everything
yet I cannot find a way,
only Zeus, to cast this dead weight of ignorance
finally from out my brain...
. . . .
Zeus, who guided men to think,
who has laid it down that wisdom
comes alone through suffering
Still there drips in sleep against the heart
grief of memory;....
From the gods who sit in grandeur
grace comes somehow violent

Grace comes violent: this brings up Zeus' power—his thunderbolts. Are they not the visible sign of the way in which intellect informs the world? We still think of the lightning flash of an idea, the spark of insight, the illumination that goes outward. Zeus is the new god of knowing and understanding who mirrors the universe in his perfect vision.

For it is the "vision" of Zeus that seems most characteristic of his mind: what the ancients spoke of as his "will," his "plan." In the *Iliad*, we are told near the beginning that the "'will of Zeus' was accomplished...by the devastation that sent strong souls of heroes to the house of Hades and gave their bodies to be the delicate feasting of dogs." The plan of Zeus—mentioned throughout the *Iliad*, was the chief theme of another epic, of which we have a fragment—the *Kypria*: "the heroes were killed in Troy / and the plan of Zeus was accomplished." The indifference of Zeus to mankind's plight I may have somewhat overdone in my beginning. But it is necessary in speaking of the Greek gods to comprehend their essential detachment, which they renounce from time to time in order to share human suffering. The *Iliad* gives ample evidence of Zeus' concern for heroes and not just the ones he propagated. Achilles, we must remember, is not of his blood—or should we say "ichor." Thetis, Achilles' mother, had very special claims on Zeus: she had released him from the shackles with which Hera, Athena, and Poseidon had bound him in the early days of his reign, when dominance on Olympos was still up for grabs. Daughter of the Old Man of the Sea, Thetis was wooed by both Zeus and Poseidon, but both cooled their ardor when Prometheus informed them that she was destined to bear a son who would be greater than his father. Zeus wanted none of that. I maintain that here is another instance, this time of restraint, where Zeus directs his amours to the furthering of the enterprise he governs. But he still maintains, apparently, his loving concern for Thetis.

Thetis, incidentally, is ubiquitous in Greek mythology. It is at her wedding to Peleus that the judgment of Paris occurs, setting the Trojan War in motion. It is she who dips her son Achilles in the river Styx, a gesture that makes him invulnerable to arrows except on the heel by which she holds him; and it is she who commissions Hephaistos to fashion the fabled shield for him, soon to die on the fields of Troy. From Zeus she extracts the promise that Achilles' honor will be vindicated by having the Achaians lose without him, down to the very borders of the beached ships, where his return will drive the Trojans back into their walled city.

Thetis goes to Zeus, asks him to bend his head if he grants her favor. Zeus regrets that he must honor Thetis' request, for it will set him in conflict with Hera; but he testifies that nothing he does is revocable; so if he does bow his head, he cannot revoke the action:

> He spoke, the son of Kronos, and nodded his head
> with the dark brows,
> and the immortally anointed hair of the great god
> swept from his divine head, and all Olympos was shaken.

Hera sees and protests. Zeus rebukes her and finally threatens her so that she withdraws in fear. An impasse seems to be reached among the gods until the crippled Hephaistos, who loves his mother and respects his father, rises to point out that a quarrel between the two about mere mortals should never disturb the tranquility of Olympos. Zeus wryly and amusedly assents, and soon the merriment and laughter of the gods resumes, drowning out the clamor of battle far below them. As Kerényi puts it, "Zeus laughs aloud; the quarrel of indestructible forms becomes a divine comedy." Immortals, we are reminded, have a much longer view of history than do those who must, however gloriously, trade their mortality for honor:

> Thereafter the whole day long [Homer tells us] until the sun went under
> they feasted, nor was anyone's hunger denied a fair portion,
> nor denied the beautifully wrought lyre in the hands of Apollo
> nor the antiphonal sweet sound of the Muses singing.
>   Afterwards, when the light of the flaming sun went under
> they went away each one to sleep in his home...
> . . . .
> Zeus the Olympian and lord of the lightning went to
> his own bed, where always he lay when sweet sleep came on him.
> Going up to the bed he slept and Hera of the gold throne beside him.

And with this final aspect of Zeus I shall close this disquisition. We have witnessed his clear mind, his intellect, his far-seeing vision by which he contemplates the entire enterprise of being, wherein the justice of Zeus assigns to each, mortal or immortal, a proper portion. We have, I trust, freed him from the charges of shallow philandering, to see that all his actions are directed to the furthering of this mighty enterprise that constitutes history. And now we see him as husband, destined by his own free will to be the mate of that singular being that is his equal, one not fearing to oppose him, reprove him, comfort him, lead him to the only bower where the *hieros gamos*, the sacred marriage, is celebrated. Here indeed is the heart of the enterprise; from it the glory that is Greek mythology ensues.

So Zeus is that spiritual faculty in all of us that knows, intuitively—not with the practical wisdom of an Athena, not with the inventiveness of a Prometheus, not with the lyric idealism of Apollo, but with a Zeusian clarity that allows things to be what they are in themselves. He knows the form of things. He is the aristocratic impulse in us, that inherent dignity of the masculine that informs mortals, both male and female, of their responsibility. He plans, wills magnificent schemes, listens, attends, watches. He loves, protects, guards. Sometimes he makes us behave tyrannically; sometimes his spirit within us turns us into philanderers; but if we attend to him properly, he teaches us that most noble of attitudes: detachment in the midst of passionate concern.

HERA
GODDESS AND WIFE

LOUISE COWAN

Hera is the most difficult of all the Olympians to comprehend. Homer depicts her as moved by such savage wrath that her consort Zeus must from time to time rebuke her. "Dear lady," he protests in Book IV,

> "... what can be all the great evils done to you
> by Priam and the sons of Priam, that you are thus furious
> forever to bring down the strong-founded city of Ilion?
> If you could walk through the gates and through the towering
> ramparts
> and eat Priam and the children of Priam raw, and the other
> Trojans, then, then only might you glut at last your anger."

Something monstrous seems to be the outcome of Hera's vengeful ire—the devouring of her enemies raw. This queen-goddess is in several ways uncomfortably close to the monstrous; Hesiod tells us that she nursed the Lernaean Hydra and the Nemean lion, both of whom Herakles has to confront in his ordeals. The most appalling account of her fury, however, is given in the Homeric "Hymn to Apollo," in which it is said that she gives birth to the monster Typhaon out of her rage against her husband. Indignant at Zeus' having borne from his own head Athena, daughter of Metis, Hera goes to the realm of the Titans, strikes the earth with her hand and prays for a child of her own, stronger than Zeus. Thus, the story goes, in time,

> she bore dreadful and baneful Typhaon, a scourge to mortals,
> whose aspect resembled neither god's nor man's.
> Forthwith cow-eyed, mighty Hera took him and, piling evil
> upon evil, she commended him to the care of the she-dragon.

Hera's mysterious and ungovernable wrath indicates a dark force that places the goddess in a different category from the other Olympian deities. She has access to a dark interiority in her own psyche; and she knows the cosmic unlit regions of gloom as well as light. The Orphic hymn addressed to her, however, views this somberness as something gracious and beneficent:

> You are ensconced in darksome hollows, and airy is your form,
> O Hera, queen of all the blessed, consort of Zeus.
> You send soft breezes ... such as nourish the soul,
> ... you nurture the winds and give birth to all.
> Without you there is neither life nor growth;
> and, mixed as you are in the air we venerate, you partake of all,
> and of all you are queen and mistress.

Hera is here conceived of as a benevolent earth goddess and "queen of all the blessed." She is present in the very air we breathe, a kind of life-spirit of nature and, as well, a ruling deity, "queen and mistress" of all. Two sets of myths are thus associated with her—those stemming from her cultic worship as earth goddess and the others from stories recounted by later collectors such as Hesiod, in which she is named in the divine genealogy as daughter to Kronos and Rhea and sister to Zeus.

Hera was originally no doubt a queen in her own right, the primeval great goddess of the Minoan people, whose way of life was matriarchal. Her first cults were probably at Argos, her temples at Samos and Olympia, and, as Jane Harrison tells us, her status as queen is marked in all her archaic representations. She became the tutelary priestess of heroes: her name is the feminine form of hero; and heroes—the spirits of dead warriors—were consecrated to her. But even early traces of the Lady (the literal signification of her name) show her to be not so much the primal earth mother as an incarnation of that divine force, powerful and independent, governing all things and retaining her connection with earth. Fulfilling the nature of woman, she is, as Bachofen has written of the feminine in general, "unable to cast off materiality, [while] the man becomes wholly removed from it and rises to the incorporeality of the sunlight."

One account has it that Zeus, the intruding young sky-god, desiring her, caused a storm to break out on Mt. Thornax, where, taking the form of a cuckoo, he flew wet and bedraggled to her breast for comfort. Out of pity, Hera tenderly received him and held him close to her bosom, where he soon resumed his true shape and characteristic demeanor. Hera insisted upon marriage to preserve her honor, and so resulted the union of earth goddess and sky god in the sacred marriage, the *hieros gamos*. When we encounter Hera among the Olympians, she has assumed a different mythic identity. She still possesses her native authority, but has allied herself with another majestic divinity—her brother Zeus, who, having deposed his father Kronos, establishes the rule of intellect in the cosmos. Kerényi speaks of the pair as "the archetypal couple whose two components belong to one another like the halves of a unity." But Hera retains her essential character in the union: each year she regains her virginity by bathing in the spring at Kanathos—a ritual that in permitting her to bestow herself afresh in marriage is a sign of her independence as well as her freedom. She does not belong to Zeus, but gives herself to him anew each year in a free act.

Thus, by the time we really come to know Hera, in Homer's *Iliad*, she has the identity of both sets of myths; but she has in effect relinquished some of her cultic status to be part of a higher society: the family of gods on Mt. Olympos. With a kind of composite identity, earth mother, sister, and spouse, Hera is the wedded consort of the father God, Zeus—but, as Kerényi points out, without herself really being the mother goddess. In fact, her role as mother is somewhat dubious: Hephaestos, Ares, and Hebe are her children, the first two considered in some sources to be her own alone, along with the monstrous Typhaon, produced parthenogenetically. Kerényi advances the idea that "the patriarchal triangle was not properly completed in the Olympian divine family.... What is missing is the 'son' who might unite this couple in a patriarchal sense as a worthy first-born."

Nevertheless, Hera is recognized as the queen of Olympos. In his hymn to her, Homer speaks of her golden throne and names her immortal queen, the most eminent of figures, the sister, "even the wife, of Zeus thunderer." Her basic equality to Zeus is acknowledged: "All the gods of Olympos revere her. They honor her *even equal to Zeus*, the lover of lightning."

The Hera of the cult had her own compelling beauty, manifested, as Pausanias tells us, in three stages of life, to conform with the phases of the moon: Hera Parthenos (the virgin); Hera Teleia (Hera Fulfilled—the wife); and Hera Chera (Hera separated from the husband). This scenario gives us a clue to Hera's autonomy: she is protagonist in her own drama, having her own quest for meaning. In her story, Hera does not exist for the male but the male for Hera.

Her status in the *Iliad*, however, seems somewhat paradoxical and even precarious. Though she is recognized as the Queen of Heaven and sits on her golden throne, she is by and large portrayed as simply one of the contending gods who take sides in the battles between the Achaians and the Trojans. Homer describes her as "white-armed," a tribute to her nobility, and "ox-eyed," a remnant of her connection with the sacred cow ceremonies at Euboeia and Boeotia; she is recognized as possessing great beauty, though she does not flaunt it and—except in one instance—seems unaware of it. This one instance is the fateful story of the golden apples, in which Paris, the Trojan prince, chooses not Hera but Aphrodite as the most beautiful among goddesses. Both Aphrodite and the other contender, Athena, are inferior to Hera in station; neither has been a goddess-queen; neither is sister and consort to Zeus. It is this affront to her honor that Hera cannot forgive. Her grudge against the Trojans and their city is one of the angers fuelling the Trojan War. Like Achilles, who also cannot overlook a slight to his honor, Hera exhibits a *cholos*, a wrath, that, though excessive, has its own nobility and fine display.

Zeus seems somewhat afraid of Hera and apparently controls her only by threats and, at least once, outright force. (Zeus once hung her by her wrists in the sky, with golden anvils at either ankle.) She accepts his authority; and his numerous amours excite her vengeance not so much against him as his sexual partners. It is her rank and station as queen and goddess that are insulted, not her sexual standing. Yet the galling effect of Zeus' infidelities remain: in her outrage Hera periodically flees to the ends of the earth to seek solitude. One of the ways in which she differs from her husband stems from her having been one of the children swallowed by Kronos, an indignity to which Zeus was not subjected. She therefore has a knowledge of the shadowy, cavernous underworld (not the chthonic region) where everything is hidden away, lost and forsaken. It is to this realm that she descends when her sense of insult proves insufferable. And it is in one of these times of seclusion that she gives birth to the monster Typhaon out of her jealousy and resentment against Metis. Hera is convinced that she should be supreme among women on all counts and is offended and vengeful if she is not given her due.

Leader of the opposition on Olympos, she is cohort of Athena on the battlefield, sponsor of the Achaeans, hater of the Trojans, maternal confederate to Hephaistos, bargainer with all the gods, jealous wife, conniving rebel, in general—or so Zeus himself seems to think--troublemaker. She has been blamed by readers for centuries for her destructive anger, her jealousy, and her deceitfulness. But the worst charge of all against her is the one made by many scholars to the effect that she has relinquished her own authority and depends only on her consort for identity. Even the great mythologist Kerényi writes, "Zeus does not need the marriage, but Hera does." What Hera needs, on the contrary, I would maintain, is an unbiased reading, avoiding the stereotypes that sometimes obscure her character.

What we have to do in order to come to terms with Hera is, as with any of the gods and goddesses: *to see the form*, in Hans Urs van Balthasar's phrase. For the clues provided by artifacts, fables, remnants of myths, comments by scholiasts, and, above all, the magnificent poems of Homer and Virgil must all be put together—and then surmounted. The spirit of a thing cannot be apprehended by the process of accumulating facts; one needs to sense the intention (the *telos*) behind the evidence. Hence, a chief clue to the interpretation of

Hera will come from Homer; for it is he who has given poetic form to the Olympian gods; and though his focus is not on Hera, one can nevertheless discern the form of Hera's mission from the shape Homer has given to his material.

For the other, hidden side of Hera's story is that, in order to be where she is, she has made an affirmation—*Fiat mihi*: "Be it done to me." And, though she rebels at times against Zeus and opposes him frequently, she never rebels against the marriage. Her *fiat* was spoken, of course, not to Zeus, but to that power over both which the Greeks called Destiny, or Fate. But there is another force connected with Fate with which Hera works—*Charis*, grace—a force that invisibly yet unmistakably reanimates events and persons and brings them to a different conclusion from the one apparently intended. Hera's way is an alternate way of doing things—that does not contradict but supplements. She has her own authority and identity, then, not so much as an earth mother image as a prefigurement of what the feminine is in its own right: not what woman was in the past but what she is to be.

Despite what one first thinks of her—that as wife she has no identity of her own and that she behaves selfishly and ignominiously—one must admit on closer examination that Hera follows deeper purposes and not just her own whims. She is in touch with something beyond the immediately visible and therefore has her own mind about things, pursuing her own prerogatives. And though she has bound herself in wedlock, she is not dependent upon a masculine world for her identity. She is complete in herself: enough to stand as an equal to almighty Zeus. Her espousal to him is both a conjugal and a sibling union, this latter establishing her equality.

Far less than the other Olympian goddesses, in fact, does she define herself in terms of the male. Athena, for instance, might be considered, as René Malamud has pointed out, a manifestation of the masculine *anima* image. And, one must admit, that great tutelary goddess is born of the masculine, chooses to be like the masculine, and does indeed excel in the masculine world—in deeds of martial valor and practical wisdom. Other feminine divinities, too, could be construed as *anima* images, arising from the depths of the masculine soul. The winsome Aphrodite relies on the pull of the erotic, the male desire for an opposite of charm and delight. Artemis exercises a strange attraction on the masculine, though she flees it, shuns it, fears it. Demeter defines herself as "other," substituting her own female cycle of fertility for any divine far-off event toward which the universe might tend.

Unlike these goddesses, Hera confronts the masculine in her own person, stands before its manifestation as herself, as the fully formed, complementary aspect of existence that does not depend on the male to confer value. Hera is the female in all its power, with political authority as well as closeness to the earth and nature. The world with which she contends is no longer a region, but the cosmos itself. She refuses to rule over a mere portion of it. A queen over all of being, she sits on a golden throne, the consort of Zeus, and cannot in any sense be construed as an *anima* figure. Hence she is the only aspect of the psyche that can make a successful marriage. She becomes, therefore, the representative goddess for anyone seriously attempting the married life.

Why do we not like her, then? First of all, precisely because she is not a projected exemplary image. She does not fit our ideas of what the model wife should be. And second, we feel distanced from her because she is not a person of relationships. She *is* in herself—and this independence is always annoying to gods and men. But can one say that she is not a person of relationships if she defines herself in marriage? So extreme a statement can be made only in light of the proposition that marriage is not a relationship; marriage is a new entity which (ideally) can take place only between two beings who are in themselves whole—and who will bring that wholeness fully to bear in a *coniunctio*, a union. When such a conjunction occurs, it initiates what Eric Voegelin has called "a leap in being": a new cosmos, a new epoch, a new polis, or a new metaphysical entity.

Hera, then, represents—she is—that other side of being which can hardly even be acknowledged in the mythological fables because it is invisible and concealed under the obvious path of the *logos*, appearing either as obstacle or as ineffectual protestation. She is *Sophia*, the feminine portion of the soul and of the cosmos, which, hidden away in darkness, unintelligible and sometimes furious, ultimately manifests itself quite discernibly by modifying, softening, delaying, altering the course of destiny. When she withdraws from Zeus, staying away from him for a year while she is pregnant with the monstrous Typhaon, we are told

> She never came to the bed of contriving Zeus
> nor pondered for him sagacious counsels
> sitting as before, on her elaborate chair
> but staying in temples where many pray ...

Her role in the marriage has been to provide "sagacious counsels." She is not simply, as Zabriskie has written, "restless matriarch in a patriarchal world." Hera is perfectly at home in her gender. As opposed to the modern concept of the second sex, gender, says Ivan Illych, "bespeaks a complementarity that is enigmatic and asymmetrical. Only metaphor can reach for it." The metaphor here is marriage, in which the complementarity, though asymmetrical, is eminently equitable. Hera has entered into a permanent partnership with the masculine as an equal, as consort and cohort, not primarily for amorous delight, though that perquisite no doubt follows (their wedding night was said to be three hundred years long) but for the completion of being and the co-creation of history.

If the gods are not only forces in the soul, but archetypes of being itself—being that is prolix, polymorphous, chaotic, contradictory, always in motion—then the quality that Hera represents is wifehood. And wifehood has had a quite negative image in the West for some centuries—perhaps from the very beginning. What gives wivery such a bad press? Is it because it has been portrayed in story and legend so frequently as little-minded, jealous, possessive, trivial, parasitical, lacking in courage, fundamentally dishonest and conniving?

Perhaps we could maintain that wifehood has been portrayed in such a way because the tellers of the tales are masculine, those chanters of the *epos* by which our culture since the Greeks has known its destiny. And we ourselves as readers are masculine in our expectations. (The spinners of other sorts of tales are feminine—the stories that tell of our old griefs and old joys and remind us of our ties to earth—folk tales, comedies, and lyrics). But the epic tale-telling is in itself logophallic; and the epic (a new kind of reality, not just a new art form, says Suzanne Langer) came into being with Zeus' reign—with the beginning of history. In this essentially masculine tale, Hera, the troublesome other half, is perceived as impediment to the ongoing of "the plan" and hence portrayed in a dubious, largely ignominious and even ludicrous light. Judged from the point of view of the story, its masculine perspective, Hera *is* unruly, possessive, a troublemaker, shrewish, vengeful. But this judgment of her actions is likely influenced by the masculine desire (the poet's and ours) to see action proceed in a straight line, observing the clear relationship between cause and effect.

Even Homer, our greatest of poets, follows the path laid down by the mythological fables, though he allows the paradoxical double action to proceed at its own pace. One stunningly beautiful passage in the *Iliad* portrays something of the splendor and mystery of the *hieros gamos*. The lyrical celebration between Zeus and Hera on Mt. Ida, even though Hera has contrived by means of it to seduce her husband away from his watchfulness of the battle, is a high point of the poem. It establishes the generative effect of their union on all the vegetative life of the cosmos. Hera has borrowed Aphrodite's loveliness and desirability (these aphroditic qualities no doubt symbolizing a distinct change from Hera's usual regal pride) for the purpose of enticing Zeus, who when he looks upon her feels desire as "a mist about his close heart as much as on that time they first went to bed together and lay in love, and their dear parents knew nothing of it." (This is a reference to one version of the story in which the two, from the beginning, are lovers.) Zeus feels a resurgence of that early love and entreats her, "Hera, ... let us go to bed and turn to lovemaking / For never before has love for any goddess or woman so melted the heart inside me, *broken it to submission* / as now"—and then he proceeds, rather ingenuously, to enumerate his many loves, including, finally, Hera herself: "not [even] yourself—" he says, "have I loved so much as now I love you, and the sweet passion has taken hold of me."

> ... the son of Kronos caught his wife in his arms.
> There underneath them the divine earth broke into young,
>   fresh grass,
> and into dewy clover, crocus and hyacinth so thick and soft it
> held the hard ground deep
> away from them.
> There they lay down together and drew about them a golden
> wonderful cloud, and from it the glimmering dew descended.

Here Homer has allowed himself to portray the generative power of the marriage bond between Zeus and Hera, showing it as an analogue to the original *hieros gamos*, in which, as the *Theogony* tells us, "great Uranus came, bringing on night and longing for love, and he lay about Gaia, spreading himself full upon her." The union of Zeus and Hera, despite their quarrels, is a genuine incarnation of the original holy marriage, and it is through this Olympian pair that the very face of the earth is renewed.

Hence, despite their bickering, Zeus and Hera represent the archetype of marriage. His promiscuity and her rebelliousness do nothing to detract from this authentic union. And what a study of the archetype makes clear is that the masculine component of this union, though serious in its commitment to the marriage, has its view fixed on the long-range plan of history: on large events that will alter the scheme of things. The masculine eros desires this vision to come about; and in order to accomplish it, must intrude into realms outside the *oikos*, away from Olympos, to produce heroes by injecting into history a bit of what Faulkner called "that Olympian ejaculation" that continually enhances and elevates the course of human destiny. In contrast, marriage is at the very heart of Hera's identity. Her inviolability is represented in the myths by the harshness with which she rejects those who dare to try to seduce her: Endymion, Ixion, Ephialtes, Otus, Ceyx. She is faithful wife to an unfaithful husband. Outrage and vindictiveness are part of the archetype; jealousy and reproaches must be accepted in the total paradigm. From the inner, hidden point of view, which makes a quite different story, Hera is pursuing her own dynamic: intuitive, wise, resourceful, tricky, passionate, following out an inner logic that gives a totally different slant to history.

Caroline Gordon perceived this different slant when she composed her novel *The Glory of Hera* in which the ending of the story shows the persecuted Herakles ascending to Mt. Olympos just after his fiery death. He is born again to a radiant Hera, in an act that completes the divine trinity (his name means "he who wins glory from Hera"). The goddess gives her amazed husband the fullest look of love she has ever given him. "Our son all along," she informs him. Virgil too perceives this obscure inner action when, in the *Aeneid* he completes Hera's story, allowing Jupiter to come to the understanding that Juno's wrath has had a higher purpose. The hated Trojans are to be allowed to found their city—though not to call it Troy, but Rome. The eternal city is to be Juno-Hera's, where she will be honored and enshrined as no other goddess. This powerful goddess' influence in human history is hidden underneath the obvious pattern of military conquest and martial display of honor; but suddenly Hera's way, the way of marriage and domestic love, is seen by a kind of reversal to be the real path, promising hope and peace for the human race.

So we have no choice but to accept her, whether we like her or not. Hera is part of the picture of reality. She leads each of us, male or female, to an understanding of the inner marriage within ourselves that makes for wholeness. She is an image of the feminine component, not in conflict with, or in comparison to, or dependent upon the masculine but working with the masculine, independently, in a kind of counterpoint. Her difficulties make possible an understanding of the ambiguity and contradiction within ourselves and enable us to see these disturbances as creative. Her headstrong certainty frees us from the tyranny of abstract reason, from senti-mentality, from erotic distractions. Our Lady brings to the process of soul-making a sternness, a counterpoint, a grace, working out in that interior *wedding feast* a movement—on a larger scale—of the soul as eternal bride.

DEMETER

GAIL THOMAS

D emeter's story tells of life's mysteries—of the secrets that comprise its growth and undergrowth. At the same time it is a tale of lament, a story of loss. It is more than the loss of a child by the mother, more than a loss of the feminine; it is a lament for the loss of the deep spiritual realms that are reached through an unbroken feminine essence. Her image is crucial to us in these times because our modern myth echoes her anguish.

Although most discussion of the Olympians begins with Zeus and Hera, Demeter is actually a much older divinity—"The eldest of the gods, the eternal and inexhaustible earth" as the chorus in Sophocles' *Antigone* calls her.

Demeter joins the Olympian ranks rather reluctantly, because within these she is diminished to the role of "Corn Goddess" or "Goddess of the Grain." In Roman times, of course, she is Ceres, whom we remember every time we walk down the cereal aisle in the grocery store. To see her great power in this way is a limitation from which we must unbind ourselves. Hers is a power more ancient, more universal than the familiar epithet, "Goddess of Agriculture." In truth, she comes before the great Olympians, and she also outlasts them.

Everyone experiences Da-Meter and has for all time in every culture. She is everywhere. "Da" is an ancient word for earth and, of course, mater or meter is both "matter" and "mother." But, it cannot be overlooked that it is in Greece that the earth-mother became particularized and worshipped in a religious event called the Eleusinian Mysteries that shaped over 2000 years of spiritual, social, and political thought and leadership. The Eleusinian Mysteries, an annual two-week ritual event honoring Demeter, continued as a source of religious initiation and worship far beyond the influence of Mt. Olympos and well into the Christian era.

To find Demeter's natural realm we must venture deep within the earth itself and be guided by the earth spirits. Her dominion is as closely associated with death as it is with life—the vegetative world and all growing things. It is in this connection with death that Demeter is always associated with her daughter, Persephone.

Demeter and Persephone cannot be separated. As image, as formidable power, as essence, they are inexorably one. Persephone's story is never complete without her connection with the mother, Demeter. As queen of the underworld, Persephone, who is sometimes called Proserpina, is married to the god Hades, and rules with him over the realm of souls. When Persephone rejoins Demeter on earth after her winter-months stay in the underworld, she brings soul-life to earth with her, impregnating the things of the world with earth spirit.

Neither Demeter nor Persephone is given an active role in the Homeric epics precisely because they are the goddesses of the chthonic realm, primordially connected to death and transformation. Like their dark sisters the Fates, the Moirai, like terrifying Medusa or red-headed Lilith (the first bride of Adam), like seductive Eve or Pandora the Beautiful Evil, Demeter and Persephone are shunned and kept at a respectful distance. As Jane Harrison points out, the heroes of the Greek epics make very hasty visits to the underworld! And yet, it is this dark side of the goddess that is ultimately the most healing. Seemingly, the wisest and most powerful among the Greeks appear to have known this to be true. For several thousand years, initiates of both sexes—the best of Greek families and highest political leaders and eventually even Roman citizens—submitted themselves to the mysteries of these two goddesses of the hidden realms.

The great Mysteries of Eleusis, conducted within the Temple of Demeter and celebrating the worship of Demeter and Persephone, were an initiation into a spiritual life unacknowledged in the daily affairs of that time. So secret were these rituals that anyone suspected of disclosing them to the uninitiated public was subject to death. Indeed, Aeschylus almost lost his life for divulging in one of his plays what the people of Athens thought was the "secret" part of the mysteries. He was attacked on the stage and only escaped by taking refuge at the altar of Dionysus. He was brought before a regular court of justice. What secrets might have prompted such allegiance? The great poet, Pindar, gives us this clue: "Happy is he who having seen these rites goes below the hollow earth; for he knows the end of life and he knows its god-sent beginnings."

The story of Demeter's lament is a longing for that which has slipped away "below the hollow earth." It is told in a solemn hymn of the 7th century B.C., "The Hymn to Demeter," in a collection now called *The Homeric Hymns*. Persephone, the beautiful daughter of Demeter, was playing in a lush meadow plucking flowers—roses and crocuses, violets, irises, and hyacinths. When she reached for the narcissus (the flower, it is rumored, that Gaia fashioned especially to lure the maiden to please the Lord of the Underworld), at that very moment the earth opened and Hades appeared in his chariot drawn by his powerful steeds. He grabbed the struggling girl and, despite her fierce fighting and loud cries, carried her down into the underworld.

Demeter heard the screams of her daughter and a "sharp pain seized her heart." She donned garments of mourning, lit a torch, and set out to search the lands of the earth. She searched for nine days and on the tenth day she encountered Hecate, but Hecate had seen nothing. Helios, the Sun God, however, had observed it all. He told Demeter that by permission of Zeus, Great Hades had abducted Persephone and had made her wife and consort to the throne of the underworld. It was a marriage that could not be dissolved.

The Homeric "Hymn to Demeter" says:

> Yet sharper pain,
> more savage even,
> struck her heart:

outraged with Zeus
wrapped in his clouds,
she withdrew
from the company of the gods
and from great Olympos,
she went to
the cities of men
and their grasslands,
disguising her beauty
for a long time.
And no one
who saw her
recognized her,
no man,
no deep-girdled
woman,
no one
until she reached the house
of prudent Celeus,
who was ruler
of the fragrant town
of Eleusis.

The daughters of King Celeus encountered Demeter when she had stopped to rest by the side of a well, disguised as an old woman. The goddess requested that she be admitted to the king's household as a serving maid. The daughters replied:

But no one of them,
after one glance,
could mistake
your beauty,
and chase you away
from the house.
No,
they would welcome you.
You look like a god.

The girls ran to their mother Metaneira, who accepted the disguised goddess and gave into her care an infant son, Demophoon Triptolemos.

For days, Deo—as the new serving woman called herself—sat by the fire in deep lament, without speaking or eating, until a bold maid named Iambe Baubo lured her into a smile with her bawdy gestures. When she was offered wine, she refused it, asking for a drink of barley flour mixed with water and the herb pennyroyal. Recognizing that this was no common nurse, Queen Metaneira was in awe of the goddess and placed everything within her household at her disposal, the great Deo's only concern to be the care of the infant son. And Demophoon "grew up like a god, without feeding at her breast, without any food at all! And they were all amazed to see the babe growing up ahead of his time."

One night, Queen Metaneira arose to spy upon the nurse and beheld Deo holding the naked infant in the flaming hearth fire. "She screamed and beat her thighs, frightened for her child, and completely outraged in her heart." The mother rushed into the room to rescue her child. And "Demeter, with her beautiful hair, was furious with her, and with her immortal hands she lifted the child out of the fire, this child whose mother bore it in the palace long after a child had ceased to be hoped for." She picked it up and threw it on the ground, her heart terribly enraged. "Stupid people, brainless, you do not even know when fate is bringing you something good or something bad. I would have made your child immortal!" And suddenly, the goddess changed her shape and size; her wrinkles vanished and her beauty shone forth; a radiant light from the immortal flesh created a brightness throughout the rooms of the palace and the royal family and all the staff fell to their knees.

Demeter ordered a temple erected above the spring where King Celeus' daughters had first met her. The great temple was erected, and there Demeter dwelled, far from the gods of Olympos, far, too, from the life of mankind. She shut herself up with the king's family and worked the magic of her terrible revenge. She made all fields unfruitful; she would not allow the seed to rise out of the earth. Here was ultimate peril to all men and beasts, but also to the gods themselves. For as men and animals could not live without plant growth, so the gods could not live without the sacrifices men offered up to them. To avert the extinction of all life, Zeus dispatched all the gods to visit the sorrowing mother and offer her the most precious gifts. But they placated neither her mourning nor her anger. "For she said she would not ever again set foot on fragrant Olympos, she would not let the fruit of the earth come up until she saw with her eyes her daughter's beautiful face."

At last Zeus was compelled to bow to her will, for otherwise all creation would have returned to dust. The earth, indeed, had lost its spirit. He sent Hermes, the "guide of souls," as a messenger to the underworld to ask the god of the shades to release Persephone. Surprisingly, Great Hades consented, saying: "Go on, Persephone, back to your mother in her black veil, go with a kind heart." But secretly, he slipped her a seed of the pomegranate and in her haste to depart, she ate it.

Accompanied by Hermes, Persephone once more stepped forth into the upper world at a moment when Demeter was looking out of her temple. "When she recognized her daughter, she leaped like a maenad in the woods on a shady mountain and ran to receive her daughter." In the midst of her joy, she stopped and asked, "My child, you should not have...the food? tell me ... so that you could come up...to live with me.... With what trick was it that the powerful He Who Receives So Many deceived you?" You see, Demeter knew the fate of anyone who ate at Hades' table—to remain one third of the year in the underworld.

Persephone confessed that, indeed, she had eaten the pomegranate seed offered to her by her husband. But Demeter's grief was overcome by the presence of her daughter. Although Demeter knew that for four months of the year, she would be without her, she took heart at the knowledge that the seed, her daughter, would be present with her for the rest of the year, replenishing the earth with its spirit.

When Zeus sent a messenger to invite mother and daughter to Olympos, Demeter, wholly reconciled, accepted the invitation. But only after she had recalled the curse of unfruitfulness from the earth and taught the kings of Eleusis how they were to celebrate in her temple the kidnapping and return of the seed corn. She taught the faithful certain rites that were never to be revealed or offended against. And she promised blessedness—a happy afterlife—to all who devoutly prayed to mother and daughter in the temple.

This version of the lament of Demeter, which I abbreviated quite radically from the Homeric Hymns, represents her image as seen from Mt. Olympos. As an image, as an archetypal presence in the world, this force we call Demeter/Persephone had undergone thousands of years of transformation by the time of Homer. According to scholars Walter Otto and Jane Harrison, much of her power has been lost in the transition of earlier matriarchal times to the patriarchal. In her earlier manifestations, she was always connected with death, as in her association in Arcadia with the Erinyes—the vengeful earth deities who upheld the ancient laws and pursued Orestes relentlessly for his act of matricide; and as the Thesmophoroi—the ancient, pre-Olympian celebrations of the harvests and first fruits. Walter Otto notes that her diminished power under Olympian rule comes about because of a change in the view of death. He says:

> The difference in thought concerning the dead is one of the most characteristic distinctions of the new religion from the old; the dead do not, indeed, cease to be, but their being is no longer that of the living and there is no longer any connection between the two spheres. Furthermore, the sphere of the dead has lost its sanctity. The gods belong wholly to life and are by their essence separated from all that is death's. The Olympian deities have nothing to do with the dead; indeed, it is expressly said of them that they shudder before the dark realm of death.... So broad is the interval that separates the Olympians from the ancient divinities.

Walter Otto goes on to say of the earlier religions:

> All of them communicate the spirit of the earth, from which derive all blessings and obligations of earthly existence, the spirit which itself gives birth to all living, and again, when life's span is over, receives it back into itself. The maternal, the feminine, occupies the prime position in this earth-bound religion. The masculine is not wanting, but it is subordinate to the feminine.

Demeter's lament is more than a mother's longing for her lost daughter. It carries the passionate desire to be connected with a realm which has been disowned and disavowed. Her actions, even in Olympian clothes, reveal a deeper knowledge of what is required for renewed vitality. Because the image is two in one—Demeter as physical life-giving forces, Persephone as spiritual, death-bringing, and life re-newing—the story carries a renewed connection to the powers of the earth, viewed in this tale as the underworld. The realm of Hades is the realm of depth—the place where experience is perceived symbolically. Hades is also Pluto the Wealthy, and therefore is god of hidden wealth—the hidden wealth of reflection, in-trospection, in-sight, in-spiration, and imagination.

Is Persephone's eating of the seed not unlike Eve's eating of the apple? These female divinities take into themselves the life spirit of the earth and become its carriers out into the world, even though that means forever altering the course of humankind by co-mingling or co-operating with the darker realms. And is it not precisely for this reason—to be forever co-mingling with the darker realms? How else is it possible to live in an en-souled world where there is life-in-death and death-in-life? Demeter/Persephone, then, engenders in us the capacity to hold the dark forces of nature. The power of Demeter keeps us close to our nurturing soul; she evokes the inner healer—the one who carries the seed of en-souled life; who releases soul into life; who accompanies life into its own depth to restore its richness, like the dream which comes to life from the underworld.

And what of Hades' consent to allow Persephone to return to the upper world? Why is it surprising? The King of Souls knows that, for there to be vitality on earth, there must be an exchange—an open channel—from the inner world to the outer world. All that is required is the planting of the seed. The Great Pluto knows his wealth will fructify the material planes even from a tiny seed.

When we separate ourselves from our soul world, we lose all capacity for life and we lose the resources for sacrifice, for "making holy" the divine nature of the world. It is in this vein that I understand Demeter's "lament." The modern term for lament is depression. Jungian analyst Patricia Berry has written extensively on Demeter's depression, deepening and expanding it to experience the mother/daughter mystery more fully. One of the literal meanings of "depressed" is "to make concave." A space is made where there was not one before, a hollow space. When we lose contact with our soul life, we become depressed, we hollow out a space to be in until a connection is again made with life-bringing forces.

This story speaks to us about the body—the body of the earth and our own body, both of which, of course, are also the mother. For both male and female, the body is the mother. This is a difficult notion, especially for men, because it asks for a total shift in perspective. But, consider it for a moment. Consider, whether you are male or female, that your body is the mother. It is Demeter. It flourishes with health and vitality. It knows what to do, because it lives harmoniously with Imagination, its indwelling spirit, which we might call Persephone and which gives health and vitality.

One day, an amazing thing happens. We lose Imagination. Persephone is simply gone from our life, and we don't know what happened to her. We mourn and grieve. Gradually, we become aware of a change in our body. It loses its freshness, its *élan*. Instead of imagining our body as the nurturing mother, imbued with gifts and resources from all of the divine forces of the cosmos, she is now simply "body"—bereft of imaginal life—left simply to cope with mundane bodily functions. We wander aimlessly in this state—pursuing health clubs, jogging partners, fad diets, vitamins, radical therapies—all hoping to bring vitality to the body from outside. Having lost the imagination of the body as mother, we women build up our muscles, slim down our thighs, and wear shoulder pads, while men ridicule the feminine and demean it, forgetting that the feminine is the healing function in the cosmos.

It is the "divine child"—the care for new life, a new idea, a project—what we might call Demophoon Triptolemos, that triggers our memory of our lost divinity, telling us our body has a divine connection to the mother.

And who or what is Hades in this scheme? Hades is the King of the Inner Realm. He is, ultimately the Inner Healer, bringing on loss and disease in order to stimulate the cyclical pattern so necessary as the healing rhythm within nature.

We cannot help but notice the small detail that Gaia "cooperates" in the abduction of Persephone by producing the narcissus flower in order to "lure" the girl to the spot where Hades would emerge from the underworld. The Homeric "Hymn to Demeter" says Gaia participates "to please Hades." The earth mother consciousness knows what it is doing, just as our body mother consciousness knows what it is doing when it produces a body symptom to "lure" us into retreat or into a different perspective where we have to ask "what wants to be seen here?"

As Karl Kerényi says, "In the symbol, the world itself is speaking!" The myths of the goddess offer images for a symbolic life that are missing in our present world. And the goddesses of the darker realms connect us once again to our original source, our primordial spirit, our inner soul-life. There is a great mystery at work here, recognized by Aeschylus when he says: "Yea, summon Earth, who brings all things to life, and rears, and takes again into her womb." Or perhaps even better said by John in his gospel, 12:24: "Verily I say unto you, unless a corn of wheat fall into the earth and die, it abideth alone; but if it die, it bringeth forth much fruit."

POSEIDON
THE GOD OF CONFUSION

DANIEL RUSS

O ne of the most intriguing and bemusing aspects of studying the Greek gods is how they defy scientific analysis and classification. An illuminating example of the gods frustrating empirical precision is the well-known statue found at the bottom of the seabed near Cape Artemísion in 1926. In fact, typical of the gods, the arm was found in 1926 and the rest of it in 1928. Even in visual images the gods refuse to be found all at once; we must pick up a piece here and a piece there. As you know, there is no consensus as to the identity of this god—some scholars call him Zeus about to hurl a thunderbolt, while others say this is Poseidon about to cast a trident. I gazed upon this image for days before I realized its meaning. Then it hit me, like a thunderbolt or like a trident: this work reveals Poseidon, the god of confusion. In the spirit of Poseidon, let me further confuse the issue by emphasizing that I am not claiming that this statue renders Poseidon. Even if Zeus is what the artist intended to portray, the reality is that Poseidon's domain, the sea, swallowed up the work for centuries, removed the one sign that could absolutely distinguish the identity, and then the sea gave it back to us as a reminder of the tensions and ambiguities that characterize the Olympian order and which are most powerfully embodied in Poseidon.

Remember that Poseidon is the elder brother of Zeus in almost every story except Homer's *Iliad*. Book 15 of the *Iliad* gives real insight into the relationship of these fraternal deities in the context of the Olympian order. Recall the scene with me when Zeus, angry at Poseidon's intrusions into the war on behalf of the Achaians, sends Iris to order Poseidon "that you quit the war and the fighting, and go back among the generations of the gods, or into the bright sea."

She then goes on to state Zeus' threat that if Poseidon disobeys, Zeus will come to fight with the "shaker of the Earth." Homer describes Poseidon's impassioned response:

> Then deeply vexed the famed shaker of the earth spoke to her: 'No, no. Great though he is, this that he has said is too much, if he will force me against my will, me, who am his equal in rank. Since we are three brothers born by Rhea to Kronos, Zeus, and I, and the third is Hades, lord of the dead men. All was divided among us three ways, each given his domain. I when the lots were shaken drew the grey sea to live in forever; Hades drew the lot of the mists and the darkness, and Zeus was allotted the wide sky, in the cloud and the bright air. But earth and high Olympos are common to all three. Therefore I am no part of the mind of Zeus.'

Having told Iris to advise Zeus to save "his blusterings and threats" for his own children, she responds most diplomatically that she will relate this strong word to Zeus, but she does wish that Poseidon would reconsider because, "The hearts of the great can be changed." Besides, she adds, "You know the Furies, how they forever side with the elder." Poseidon concedes to her wisdom saying:

> Now this, divine Iris, was a word quite properly spoken. It is a fine thing when a messenger is conscious of Justice. But this thing comes as a bitter sorrow to my heart and my spirit, when Zeus tries in words of anger to reprimand one who is his equal in station, and endowed with destiny like his.

We will take up Poseidon's final message to Zeus later, but for now we will reflect on what this passage reveals about Poseidon's image of himself and his relationship to Zeus. He acknowledges Zeus as the king of the gods, but denies that he is inferior in any sense to Zeus. They simply have different domains. Walter Otto says that this episode and other Homeric descriptions of Poseidon "indicate that his true greatness belongs to the past" and that "he appears to be somewhat awkward and old-fashioned" before the younger deities. While this may be true of the way Homer revisions Poseidon, I believe that this portrayal is consistent with Poseidon's character, for he is a god who defies the status quo and exists to shake up the predictable, while Zeus, Hesiod tells us, "who in his wisdom assigned to each of the gods their properties and settled their privileges," is compelled to order and organize and govern everything. It is this distinction between Zeus who wants to settle everything and Poseidon who wants to shake things up that makes Homer call Poseidon younger than Zeus. For he is older in that he embodies a pre-Olympian order that thrives on flux, and he is younger in that it is a mark of the young to celebrate the rush of life with its flood of experiences.

This celebration of flux, fusion, and confusion characterizes Poseidon from this our first knowledge of him. He is *Poteidan*: meaning master, lord, or husband of Da, one of the early names for Demeter. He loves her before she is given a new name among the Olympians. Hence his surname Gaiaochos, meaning "husband of earth." But he is not merely associated with loving Gaia, the Great Mother, but with loving Demeter, the fecund, fertile goddess of the death and rebirth of vegetative life, of the dark earth and the dark underworld. This is a far more fluid image of the earth than the Great Mother since it captures the image of Earth's life flowing through and then withdrawing from vegetative life in the ebb and flow of seasons. And it is no surprise how Poseidon unites with Demeter, as Karl Kerényi describes it:

> It was told that when Poseidon began to pursue Demeter with amorous importunities, the goddess was already engaged in seeking her abducted daughter Persephone. Demeter turned herself into a mare and mingled with the grazing steeds of King Onkios. Poseidon perceived the trick, and coupled with Demeter in the shape of a stallion. The wrathful goddess turned into Erinys, the goddess of anger, and was actually called Demeter Erinys until she washed away her anger in the river Ladon....

Kerényi goes on to tell of their offspring, a daughter whose name might not be spoken outside the Mysteries, and the famous steed Arion. He had many other stallion marriages—he is a violent lover—one of which was with Medusa, giving birth to Pegasus.

While Poseidon shares with many gods the deep connection with the bull, it is Poseidon's distinction to be the giver and tamer of the wild horse. Chronologically, whatever that means to the gods, our oldest rumors of Poseidon come from Eurasia, from the Arian peoples who eventually invaded and settled southern Greece. Charles Seltman, in an attempt to rationalize the Greek gods, nonetheless gives an illuminating description of the presence of Poseidon among them:

> Dwelling in an area of wide pasture-lands, these Aryan peoples succeeded in domesticating the wild horse of the Eurasian steppes and invented the wheel. Consequently, when ultimately they found themselves driven to migration because they were multiplying too quickly, they were able to break out of their confines to overrun vast regions of the habitable globe at a speed far greater than had ever previously been possible to any wandering races and nations. [Note what he says next.] Possessed of locomotive animals and wheeled transport, they became a wagon-dwelling culture which moved in search of pasture-lands.... Theirs was the earliest big 'folk-wandering' for which we have historical evidence, and numerous others have occurred since, always bringing disaster to the occupants of the invaded lands, the latest example being one of the most romantic of recorded adventures, the movement of the covered wagons across the great plains of the American continent last century.

Seltman then concludes: "it is possible to say that the [Aryans] brought four things with them [to Greece]: wheeled vehicles, the art of producing wheel-made pottery, the horse, and their chief god—himself apt to be equine—Poseidon."

While we will ignore the implication that one can explain away the gods as a primitive deification of technological advancement, I want us to attend to remythologizing this historical account. It reveals much about Poseidon and his relationship to human culture. It reminds us that he is first the tamer of horses before he is the savior of ships. He first gave man horse power, freeing us for locomotion on a massive scale. We know of these deep sexual associations with the power of the steed, this bestial and spirited presence in the loins of civilization. And we remember the transcendent aspiring of the human spirit which binds each of us to the flight of Pegasus. But Seltman suggests to us that in the gift and presence of Poseidon we find a resource to reflect our Wanderlust, that insatiable human desire which we usually blame on necessity to restlessly traverse the earth. The intrigue with getting in the car and just driving. The eros that we feel at the prospect of a train ride to no place in particular, and the impulse to go somewhere, anywhere as we move with the flow of the masses at the airport, waiting to pick up a friend. It is this desire to know life's surge and fluidity on a massive scale, this locomotivation that is the gift of Poseidon. And it is dangerous to the stability of civilization. As Charles Segal puts it in a discussion of Euripides' *Hippolytus*: "Both Poseidon and Eros embody forces outside civilization which civilization is forced, with pain to recognize." Unlike Zeus who gives mankind a vision of order or Prometheus who endows these creatures of a day with gifts to multiply and subdue the earth, such things do not concern Poseidon. He is the father of Polyphemos and patron god of that realm of the nomad and barbaric cyclops who simply live off the flow of nature, eating whatever or whomever they find in the flow of existence. And he is the patron god of the Phaiakians, those people who live no place in particular and who exist to be a convoy without hurt to all men. They embodied the very nature of Poseidon, being a utopia never settled enough to be mapped, thriving on flux, and moving strangers on when they come. Poseidon's judgment against them is that they conveyed one man too many when they aided his enemy Odysseus in his journey home. Not only did Poseidon seek to thwart the homecoming of Odysseus because of his sacrilege against the Earth Shaker, but Poseidon is not a god particularly partial to homecomings of any sort, since they entice men to settle down.

This title of Earth-shaker is, I believe, deeply rooted in Poseidon's passion for locomotion. Some scholars have tried to associate Poseidon with earthquakes caused by volcanoes on the Greek peninsula. But there is no proof that the Greeks connected earthquakes and volcanoes and Poseidon. It is more likely that Poseidon as earth-shaker derives from his presence and power in and through both horses and later, water, which not only shake the very surface of the earth, but also cause floods of invading and wandering peoples to roam the earth, shake up prevailing societies, and confuse cultures. Poseidon loves it when the Greeks invade Troy, not because he wants them to vindicate their honor, return home, and settle down, but because the Trojans have insulted him and he wants to shake the very foundations of their civilization. But he gets no less pleasure from thwarting the homecoming of thousands of Greeks and is appeased to find out that, while the gods demand Odysseus' safe return to refound Ithaka, the old hero will give his body up to the god of the sea in the end. There will be no place to honor him.

What about this rather late change in Poseidon as god of the Sea? He tells us in the passage we read earlier from the *Iliad* that this was allotted him after the overthrow of Zeus and the founding of the Olympian order. But there are deeply rooted connections with the springs of the earth in stories that seem pre-Olympian. Robert Graves suggests that: "Horses were sacred to the moon, because [we might say therefore] their hooves make a moon-shaped mark, and the moon was regarded as the source of all water; hence the association of Pegasus [and I would add Poseidon] with springs of water." Again we have this profound connection to the flux of existence. And springs move the earth from within not only to give forth vegetation but to move the soil and rocks along so the earth is forever being formed. Poseidon brings this memory to us through his springs of water.

Perhaps the most striking example of Poseidon's connection to the earth through water is that of his contest with Athena when both were vying to become the patron deity of Athens. In order to convince the gods that his patronage could best guide Athens, he threw his trident into the rock atop the acropolis, and withdrawing it, three rivulets of fresh and salt water began to flow, which became the fountain of Lerna. Athena caused the olive tree to grow and, of course, the gods voted her the winner and, to Athens' great joy, she became their patron deity, not Poseidon. Outraged, Poseidon sent huge waves to flood the Thriasian plains where later Athens would be built. In various ways, the Athenians were careful thereafter to honor Poseidon.

But this association with saltwater and flooding is not the essence of the god of the sea. Gaston Bachelard (quoting Charles Ploix) reflects that:

> Poseidon, then, belongs to fresh water. It is fresh water in general because the waters, scattered in a thousand springs over the country, all have 'their fetishes.' In his first generalization, Poseidon is consequently a god who generalizes the gods of springs and rivers. By associating him with the sea, people only continued this generalization.

Bachelard insists that the sea is a dead thing to the human imagination, except when connected with the fresh life-giving sources from which it springs and to which it will return in the cycles of rain. So it is no accident that this divine presence who embraces earth in the flow of life, who gives the horse so that peoples might surge through the earth and shake its civilizations, who gives springs to remind us of the fluidity and flux beneath the seemingly unshakable foundations of all our Athens, it is no accident that he should take for his domain the water that embraces the whole earth, the seas that incessantly reshape her boundaries, the oceans that carry the ships teeming with peoples of the sea who unsettle the civilized world, and that domain where the numbers and relationships of the deities is most confused.

ATHENA
GUARDIAN OF WHOLENESS

DONA S. GOWER

The figure of Athena inevitably evokes awe. Although she is described by Homer and others as the "ever near," she seldom appears merely to provide comfort for those she loves. Indeed, in her first visitation to Achilles in the *Iliad*, Athena of the "terrible eyes" grabs the enraged hero by the hair of his head in order to force him to refrain from killing Agamemnon. Athena's immediate involvement in the lives of heroes reflects her mission—and her quality—to bring right-mindedness into the realm of action in the world. In peace and war, she provides wise counsel for men and for gods, the kind of counsel that results in good judgment and proper conduct. Like Prometheus, she educates men and thereby elevates them to god-like states so that they can bring the future into flower. Of this characteristic, Walter Otto has written:

> What Athena shows man, what she desires of him, and what she inspires him to, is boldness, will to victory, courage. But all of this is nothing without directing reason and illuminating clarity. These are the true fountainheads of worthy deeds, and it is they which complete the nature of the goddess of victory. This light of hers illumines not alone the warrior in battle: wherever in a life of action and heroism great things must be wrought, perfected and struggled for, there Athena is present.

In poetic depictions, Athena stands out as perhaps the only Olympian whose integrity never wavers under the influence of *eros* or jealousy. Her image in art and poetry always suggests a serene self-containment that makes her a powerful tutelary figure when she addresses either men or gods. And in her battle gear, with the Gorgon's head on the aegis, her imposing figure brooks no opposition.

The story of Athena's birth perhaps contains the secret of her extraordinary power. In his monograph *Athene*, Karl Kerényi has suggested that her name, obscure in its etymological origins, may mean "sacred vessel," "receptacle," or, in its oldest form, "pan." In one sense, this name suggests her ability as the receptive principle to embody both the masculine and feminine powers in being itself. The Homeric Hymn describing her birth makes explicit the intimidating effect of the advent of such a figure. She emerges from the head of Zeus, who had swallowed her pregnant mother (Metis or Council), uttering a war whoop. This newly-born goddess is fully developed as a female, even though she is clad in masculine armor. The poet tells us that:

> Great Olympos itself
> shook terribly
> under the might
> of bright-eyes,
> the earth groaned
> awfully and the ocean
> was moved to foam up
> with dark waves,
> then as sudden
> the salt sea stopped.
> The glorious son of Hyperion,
> the sun, stood
> his fast-footed horses still
> for a long time,
> until the girl
> took that god-like armor
> from her immortal shoulders.

If the gods themselves are stricken with fear, their reaction indicates that the presence in one being of such a confluence of complementary masculine and feminine qualities evokes a sense of the original unity about which Plato speaks in the *Symposium*.

In that dialogue Plato provides Aristophanes, the great comic poet, the opportunity to explain that human beings were at first androgynous. His story describes the gods' fear that the power of such an entity might threaten Olympos itself. To prevent the usurpation of the gods by this new creature, the Olympians split the original human being into different sexes. Aristophanes thus accounts for *eros* as "nothing more than the name for the desire and pursuit of the whole" that the original unity embodied.

Thus, with the birth of Athena, the myth of unity is extended to include even the gods. Indeed, the relationships among the Olympian deities suggest an essential complementarity between separate powers. Athena stands out, in contrast, as the imaginative embodiment of the whole soul—human and divine—in all its elements. She alone is self-contained. Zeus needs Hera for completion—even though the swallowing of Athena's mother, Metis, provided him with the indwelling of the feminine that would inform his judgments and make him *polymetis*. Athena is the incarnation of the unified soul and, therefore, does not require completion in the metaphor of the sexual union between male and female. She springs from Zeus' head a complete embodiment—a female form dressed in war gear, guardian and protector, a sacred vessel that gives birth to and protects the *polis*.

Athena's emergence has further cosmic implications. Her coming makes the "earth groan...awfully" and the ocean "foam up with dark waves" and then stop entirely in a moment of contemplation that both disturbs and arrests simultaneously. Even the sun "stood his fast-footed horses still for a long time"—thereby stopping the movement of history itself—until this dazzling new presence takes "that god-like armor from her immortal shoulders." Earth, air, water, and fire seem strangely subordinated to and yet incarnated in the divine image of the virgin protector of cities (Athena *Polias*) whose martial aspect threatens enemies in order to be salvific, to guard, to bring peace out of war.

On the shield of Achilles in the *Iliad*, Athena is linked with Ares in the work of war, but her willingness to be the destroyer of cities

(Athena *Persepolis*) stands in sharp contrast to that of the bloody Ares. Only when her sense of justice is provoked does she unleash a menacing power that sometimes unites with the chaotic and brute force of the war god himself. The "terrible Pallas Athena" with the Gorgon's head on her aegis at such times can admit and aid the fury of destruction—even in cities which have apparently honored her in their sacred precincts. Because the Trojans acquiesce in Paris' abduction of Helen, Athena will not look with favor on the sacrifices offered in her temple at Ilium. But, unlike her brother Ares, who cares not for the justice of a cause but only for winning, Athena's terrible qualities are let loose only on those cities ceasing to function under the right aegis and, therefore, deserving of retributive justice. Hence, the integrity that Athena's person represents must be maintained within the breasts and citadels of those who honor her.

In the destruction of Ilium, for example, a city housing her Palladium, the goddess allows her own temple to be the scene of retributive violence against the Trojans. The chorus in Euripides' *Trojan Women* expresses its terror at the apparent coldness emanating from the just goddess who allowed the Trojan horse into the temple, the "house of Pallas Athene stone paved, washed now in the blood of our people." Yet in permitting this act—paradoxically both violation and sacrilege of her temple and, at the same time, the violence underlying sacrifice—she judges the performers. If the Trojans have deserved the destruction of their city, Athena's favorites, the Achaeans, go beyond the bounds of justice in their bloody slaughter of Priam and his family on sacred ground. For this crime, Athena wishes to make the Achaeans' homecoming sorrowful, even in the victory she has helped to achieve. The aftermath of this slaughter will include the death of Agamemnon when he returns to Argos in hybristic triumph. Even her beloved Odysseus, because of his alienation of Poseidon, will go his many-turning ways for another ten years before reaching Ithaka and his longed-for mate, Penelope.

Athena brings about her hero's safe return in the *Odyssey* in the context of bringing a new order to faction-ridden Ithaka. This city has had no real leader since Odysseus' departure for Troy. In restoring the leader, she saves Ithaka from the self-seeking ravages of the plundering suitors who have been vying for Penelope's hand. Yet Athena must also enlist the power of the other Olympians in order to achieve her aim without arousing Poseidon's antipathy. She maneuvers in the council held on Olympos, not in direct affront to Poseidon but in subtle advantage, seizing the moment in which confrontation is not likely, to prepare the way for Odysseus' homecoming and for the placation of the god. Indeed, Athena waits until Poseidon has gone to Ethiopia for a banquet in his honor before approaching Zeus. Athena also precedes her hero to Ithaka so that she can initiate Telemachos into manhood and thereby guarantee that Odysseus will have a worthy son to stand by him when the hall is to be purged of the suitors.

Even after Odysseus has achieved his *nostos*, or homecoming, and been reunited with his wife and with the son the goddess has mentored, Athena's presence ensures that the hero should not carry vengeance too far in retaliation against the suitors' kin. When Odysseus exults in a murderous impulse to pursue "like a high-flown eagle" those who seek retribution for his slaying of the suitors, Athena commands him to "hold hard, stop this quarrel in closing combat, for fear / Zeus of the wide brows, son of Kronos, may be angry with you." Odysseus obeys, we are told, "with happy heart." This hero, whose wise counsel identifies him with the goddess, will later make a final journey of expiation for his offense to Poseidon in order to set up the worship of this god in a place so far inland that people do not know the sea. Hence Athena's guiding presence demonstrates her ability once more to placate even in victory those opposing forces that could destroy the commonweal of the *polis* as well as the hero himself.

Athena's role as teacher or guardian is thus essential in the story of her relationship with both Odysseus and his son Telemachos. But her protection and tutelage—albeit in court—of Orestes, who is referred to throughout the *Odyssey* as a model for Telemachos' own growth into manhood, further underscores the power of the goddess to reconcile apparent opposites.

Though Aeschylus would not write the *Oresteia* until several hundred years after Homer's epics of the Trojan war and its consequences, the fifth-century tragedian insisted that his work was but "a cold slice off of Homer's banquet." This sole surviving trilogy recounts Agamemnon's return and death, the murder of Clytemnestra by her son Orestes at Apollo's behest, and the working out of divine and human justice amidst conflicting claims of right and wrong. Aeschylus portrays Athena in the final play as the paragon of wise counsel, *polymetis*, the daughter not only of the father but of the feminine principle as well, who alone can resolve warring deities as masculine and feminine forces in the *polis* which if not in harmony can rend it apart. Athena reminds the Furies of her power when she tells them in the *Eumenides* that she alone knows where Zeus' thunderbolts are kept. But she relies not on the intimidation of might but on the power of *Peithos* (Persuasion, also a feminine goddess) to bring about genuine reconciliation.

Athena takes the stage in the *Oresteia* as the presiding presence on the Acropolis, her own citadel in Athens, where Orestes has sought sanctuary, clasping the knees of the goddess' statue in supplication. In Walter Otto's words, the "great thing which must be wrought and struggled for," will be the just city in which the very principles of wholeness she embodies are realized. Athena tells Orestes and the Furies who have pursued him about the nature of her sacred soil: "This is the place of the just. Its rights forbid / even the innocent to speak evil of his mates." On the Areopagus, she instructs the twelve men of Attica whom she summons to help judge the case between Apollo/Orestes and the Furies to hear her decree: "For Aegeus' population, this forevermore / shall be the ground where justices deliberate." This ground, again, is that foundation of the *polis* wherein and whereon the cosmic and earthly forces have striven for dominance and sought for habitation: "Here is the hill of Ares, here the Amazons / encamped and built their shelters when they came in arms / for spite of Theseus, here they piled their rival towers / to rise, new city, and dare his city long ago, / and slew their beasts for Ares. So this rock is named / from then the Hill of Ares." But the Areopagus takes at this point in civilization a new meaning in which a peaceful balance, not war, is achieved.

Though Athena herself casts the deciding ballot in an otherwise equally divided jury, she nonetheless makes her chief business the placation of the ancient forces, predating the new Olympian gods, who deserve recognition in the *polis* even though they come from deep within the earth and represent the powers of the feminine to exact, in unending replication, blood restitution. She transforms the Furies through *Peithos* (persuasion) into *Eumenides* (kindly ones), who instead of civil strife and war bring benisons to the city which honors their feminine presence. Athena comments: "Strong guard of our city, hear you these / and what they portend? Fury is a high queen / of strength even among the immortal gods / and the undergods, and for humankind / their work is accomplished absolute, clear: / for some, singing; for some, life dimmed / in tears; theirs the disposition." She knows that this awful power, like her own, should be feared even in beneficence, for the destructive force is awakened by the careless soul. These ladies pray that Civil War will not fatten on men's ruin and urge the *polis*: "Let love be their common will; / let them hate with single heart. / Much wrong in the world thereby is healed." This paradigm for wholeness, expressed in the *Oresteia*, is particularly appropriate for the city of Athena *Parthenos*. The virgin "receptacle" of all that is sacred in the cosmic powers is also the virgin mother of the people named for her. The Furies' final benison points to the civilizing effects of the balance that her presence creates in the city: "Farewell citizens / seated near the throne of Zeus, / beloved by the maiden he loves, civilized as years go by, / sheltered under Athena's wings, / grand even in her father's sight."

In the comic vein, Aristophanes provides a final image of Athena, though she is not literally present in his play *Lysistrata*. At a time when Athens had declined from its former glory, when Greek fought with Greek—Spartan against Athenian—yet claimed to worship these same eternal presences, the comic playwright sets the scene of a comic resolution to strife on the Acropolis. Like the historical priestess of the Virgin goddess, the heroine of this play is married, and she brings to the Parthenon women from all over Greece to unite in a bloodless battle of the sexes for the health and balance of a civilization that has grown too masculine. In withholding sex, they appropriately occupy the protected space of the virgin. Yet their movement is toward a consummation that this Virgin's own person embodies. The final action of the play sings of the reunion of the spouses and of the balanced peace in which Spartans and Athenians sing each other's praises.

The women, as Lysistrata tells the men, have woven—as the Greeks did for Athena at her great festival—a new cloak of state which, like Athena's peplum, will incorporate the feminine and masculine, softening the aggressive and calling for a rule of law informed by love. Athena's sacred helm in this play represents the sacred vessel her name implies. One of the women uses it to look pregnant and escape to her husband before the treaty has been accomplished. When discovered, she insists to Lysistrata that she is pregnant and has taken the sacred helm "so if the throes should take me / Still in these grounds I could use it like a dove / as a laying nest in which to drop the child." This goddess who does not herself bear children is nonetheless the sacred vessel, then, not only for the masculine principle but for all the children of the *polis*. She provides the nest, external to herself but correlative to her own containment, which nurtures and protects and teaches. Like the basket bearing Ericthonios, the very hidden child, during Athena's festival, the helm of war is transformed by Aristophanes into a protective receptacle for the *polis* she guards.

The last lines of the play—hilarious songs invoking all the gods—chant the invocation of Athena of the House of Brass, the divine presence worshipped in Sparta, whose universality resides in any civilized undertaking that strives for perdurability. The great Helen is invoked to "sing praise to the warrior goddess templed i' our lands, / her o' the House of Brass." This play, then, also celebrates Athena's triumph in the *Iliad* and *Odyssey*. Athena is given credit for restoring the captured Queen to her rightful land, thereby, making Menelaos whole, and for providing the necessary feminine presence in the endeavors of civilization.

No wonder, then, that Athena stands as mentor to us all and gives urban life her patronage in all the arts. Combining Promethean foresight with Zeusian order and law, Athena, like the goddess Hera (with whom she plots disobedience to Zeus in the *Iliad*), knows that her function is completion. Karl Kerényi has spoken of Athena's embodiment as a powerful creation with its dualities held in para-doxical tension and affirmation: "The image was created from a depth of artistic praxis where the divine forms are experienced directly and not cogitated." So Athena leads the world to her image. She is fully cognizant that, in knowing her image, civilization knows as well not only her great father but all of the presences—old and new—that history embraces and that engender civilized life.

ARTEMIS

EILEEN GREGORY

Potnia potnia semnotata—thus Hippolytus summons his goddess Artemis—*kallista polu parthenon*. When we think of Artemis we generally imagine the *kallista polu parthenon*—the loveliest of virgins. She is the one who, as Hippolytus says, dwells "in an inviolate Meadow. / No shepherd dares to feed his flock within it: / no reaper plies a busy scythe within it: / only the bees in springtime haunt the inviolate Meadow.... Reverence [*aidos*—shame, modesty] ... refreshes it with water from the river." We should try to understand this image of divine girlhood wrapped around in purity and modesty—the image of Artemis promulgated by Homer and most loved by poets and artists. But we need to go beyond it too. Even Hippolytus' own words—much against his conscious intention—suggest more than the untouched virgin. They indicate as well Artemis' connection with the exotic Aphrodite: in Greek literature aphroditic kinds of things (seductions, rendezvous, rapes) happen in secluded meadows lush with flowers. Also unconsciously, Hippolytus suggests his own connection with another *parthenos* out picking flowers—Persephone, violently initiated into sexuality and death. As Hippolytus says, Artemis is *semnos*. Like the goddesses of the Eleusinian mysteries, and like the dreaded Furies, she is *potnia semnotata*—mistress most terrible and holy. To understand Artemis' divine image we need somehow to see that grace and loveliness most rendered by the poets, together with the awesomeness revealed in her cults of worship. In fact, one can fully understand that virginal grace only in seeing its gravity and portent. For Artemis, though virginal and bright, often exists in a charged erotic climate and at the boundary of the underworld.

Artemis' worship in Greece, according to Lewis Farnell, was

more prevalent and widespread than that of any other goddess. One wouldn't know this from Homer, whose depiction of her as a sweet little thing dancing with a bunch of girlfriends is slight and, in terms of the tradition of her worship, remarkably narrow, suggesting only in an elegant and oblique way the intensity, darkness, and even savagery that often attended her cults. Homer suppresses the nimbus of ancient associations surrounding Artemis and presents her as the archetype of Girlhood, Tomboyishness, just before it moves toward the inevitable bonds of marriage. More serious goddesses at that point take over, as Athena does with Nausicaa in the *Odyssey*, or as Hera traditionally does in the marriage rite itself, and Aphrodite in the marriage chamber. This ephemeral girlhood for the Greeks was fairly brief, since women married at the age of thirteen to fifteen. One suspects that this conception, Eternal Girlhood, is a deliberate trivialization, especially considering the enormity of Artemis' ties to the Great Goddess. It gives Artemis control of a small and diminished portion of female destiny, itself valuable only in relation to its loss in serving the institution of marriage.

The image created by Homer—the virgin huntress, shy, graceful, and tender, but inept in serious matters (like war), sweet daughter to Leto and sweet sister to Apollo—is the one that has held most favored status in subsequent literary tradition. But her association with Leto and her twinship with Apollo speak to only a small part of her significance. According to Farnell, she was worshipped in conjunction with her mother or her brother fairly seldom; and though she is generally known as the Virgin Goddess in literary tradition, she was never worshipped *as virgin*, with the title *parthenos* in cult. Her virginity is not a primary cultic significance, and her affiliation with the most ancient and potent of goddesses suggests a broader, more chthonic dimension of power. Aeschylus calls Artemis the daughter of Demeter, and in worship, Farnell demonstrates, she is associated through cultic epithets with one or another goddess who is *potnia semnotata*—the Korai, Aphrodite, Hecate, the Fates, and the Furies, Nemesis, and Adrastea. Artemis's depiction as Huntress gives some suggestion of ominous connections, pointing to her inexorable ruthlessness, which can be turned on mortals as well as upon animals. The Homeric "Hymn to Artemis" states: "The crests of tall mountains / tremble, and the thick-shaded forest resounds / dreadfully with the cries of beasts, while the earth / and the fishy deep shudder. Hers is a mighty heart, / and she roams all over destroying...."

In religious terms Artemis is by no means the simplest of the Olympians, but rather confusing and contradictory. As an image of aspects of human experience she is bewildering. Yes, I mean, really, *bewildering*. Because suddenly that word seems generously given as a clue—so allow me to muse on it. *To bewilder*: to cause to lose one's bearings, to perplex or confuse through want of a plain path. *To wilder*: to lead astray, to wander, to revert to the wild. *Wild*: living in a state of nature, not tame or domesticated or cultivated; flourishing without the aid of man; savage; impatient of, or not subjected to, restraint; eager with desire, erratic. *Wilderness*: from Anglo-Saxon, meaning literally, wild-deer-ness: a tract uncultivated and uninhabited by human beings—a pathless waste. One notes that wildness and wilderness are defined in negatives, in relation to civilization; that to be wildered or bewildered is measured in terms of the path, the known demarcation. To be pathless, without a clear path, or to be led astray or wander from the path is to be lost, to be in a barren waste.

In all her varying aspects Artemis lies in this territory of the wild, as opposed to the civilized—or rather, one might say, she is manifest at the outer edges of the civilized and the rationally knowable. In this role as a fierce guardian of boundaries she is like her brother Apollo: her presence at the thresholds of civilization sets an absolute limit, defining by strict and overwhelming retribution those actions that transgress—actions of violent possessiveness and aggression, concomitant with civilized habits that see the world in terms of mastery.

Artemis is rarely if ever a city goddess. Unlike Athena or Hera, Farnell points out, she has nothing to do with political or intellectual life. She does not, like the other Olympian goddesses, have any major role in the institution of marriage or of the family. It is true that Artemis oversees the perils of childbirth; she may grant women or young girls painless rather than tortured death; and she nurtures the growth of the young. But these roles pertain not to seminal order (semen/polis/logos, the preservation of the male line, the production of heroes) but to the territory of natural survival—the goddess in relation to the woman or child in the austere loneliness of danger, pain, and death. This inexorable domain is echoed in her protection of hunters, who enter wild territory to survive by strength or skill.

Artemis nurtures the undomesticated, untamed, that which flourishes without human intervention, and within an order alien to human concerns. From the perspective of civilization, she signifies that which is radically and excessively outside the power of human manipulation, and therefore her territory seems threatening and uncanny.

Artemis is the goddess of virgin wilderness—goddess of wild beasts, fowl, and fish (*potnia theron*), both their protector and their ruthless slayer. And she is the goddess of numinous forests and of still and running waters. Her Greek temples, according to Vincent Scully, are located in overwhelming, uncanny landscapes, in deep valleys or depressions, the axis of worship lined up with a powerful, cone-shaped peak, or with twin peaks, with tumuli or clefts—images of the ancient Great Goddess. This is the dreadful goddess, associated in Greek imagination with the taboo of human sacrifice. She is the goddess of Aulis, part of the net of Nemesis and the Fates and Furies in the Trojan War. While the Greeks are idled at Aulis before the war, Artemis sends a portent, two eagles feasting on a hare carrying unborn young. The seer interprets the portent: "Artemis the undefiled / is angered with pity / at the flying hounds of her father / eating the unborn young in the hare and the shivering mother. / She is sick at the eagles' feasting." Artemis demands of Agamemnon that he slaughter his own innocent child Iphigenia before he can sail to Troy to slaughter other innocent victims in pitiless violence.

Walter Burkert indicates that in Greece both hunters and warriors, in rituals initiating their action of slaying, evoked Artemis and reenacted virginal sacrifice, a ritual gesture of masculinizing the heart, making the heart hard for the action of slaughter. Yet paradoxically Artemis is also the protector of the wild and of the young. The myths surrounding her suggest retribution for a hardness of heart that leaves pity behind. Within this paradox of Artemis' ruthlessness and pity is an unspoken law, a hidden human necessity—that the slayer, acknowledging his own vulnerability and the gift of his life, identify with the slain.

Artemis guards that which is untouched by man's hands—not only the virgin wilderness but, in human terms, the young virgin not yet marriageable, belonging to herself, full of delicacy, play, freedom, and grace of movement, yet having moments of stillness and quiet that intimate deep interiority. That quiet inwardness and unselfconscious dignity is a gift granted to a woman of any age—thus in the *Odyssey*, not only the young girl Nausicaa is like Artemis, but Penelope, Helen, Arete, Kalypso, and Circe also possess her youthful grace.

But just as the wilderness is defined negatively in terms of civilization, the untouched virgin, in Greek thought, exists to be touched; the inviolate is a function of violation, which serves the political function of procreation. The unwed woman is uncultivated, flourishing apart from civilized usefulness, her wildness needing to be tamed. Thus, in Greek mythology, the inviolate virgin is open game; one notes continual acts of rape and attempted rape against Artemis and her maiden followers, coming from the lust to possess the unpossessable. And Artemis exacts her due against the aggressor: thus the terrible retribution against Acteon, Orion, and others, who bring their own violence home to their own violated bodies. Manifest in brilliance at the boundary of the wild and the civilized, Artemis in a sense mirrors back upon the transgressor the violent lust inherent in the will to master and tame.

Having sketched something of the mythic configuration associated with Artemis, one might ask what these Artemisian images signify in contemporary life. It is not easy in contemporary life to locate the wilderness, which disappears relentlessly like a mirage on our ghostly satellite maps. And in our ecological concern for wilderness, do we know the wilderness *as wild*, or rather as already tamed within the Wordsworthian sentimentality of our nostalgia? And after Freud's morbid and crazy explication of the Taboo of Virginity and other musings on the polymorphous sexual perversity of the child, we are somewhat at a loss to understand or to give place to Artemis' austere and quiet untouchableness.

But at least, in the devastation of our century, we begin to recognize the ominousness and blindness of the civilizer's gaze toward the wilderness. Susan Griffin imagines the American discoverer of virgin land:

> He is the first. Truly he has come farther than any man before him. His eyes have beheld what has not been seen before. What newness he is blessed with, what freshness! None of the beauty of this land has been brought down, no part soiled. He is the first to tread here. Only the mark of his shoes effaces the soil. Pine. Otter. Canyon. Musk ox. She gives up her secrets. He is the first to know, and he gives names to what he sees. He records the existence of these things. He is thinking to preserve these moments for posterity. He draws a map of his way across this land. And he charts the shape of the place. Behind the mountain range. On the other side of the valley. Down the riverstream. Across the gorge. He finds the unknown irresistible. He believes what is hidden in this land calls to him. He feels undiscovered grasses tremble in wait for him, he imagines mysterious lakes glistening revelation, he knows there are meadows, ignorant of his being, which will open to him.... And the wilderness embraces him. He is taken up by wildness. He becomes wild. Now the secrets of the place are his and each of his footsteps is a triumph.

This eye gazes and measures in terms of what can be possessed, known, appropriated. Thus, though the man becomes wild, his wildness serves only to instrument his complete ownership. It is wildness only as willful excess—and ripe for retribution.

Curiously, the Canadian experience of the wilderness has been quite different from the American. Such sanguineness as this—a confidence in the acquiescence of the virgin land to the touch—was never possible to the Canadian explorer or settler. In Canada one could not entertain the illusion of the compliance of the wilderness, there so overwhelmingly more powerful than the human. One Canadian writer, Margaret Atwood, has said that the imaginative presence shaping the life of Canada was never maternal but always virginal—Dark Persephone or Hecate—or, I would say, ancient Artemis, *potnia theron*, mistress of beasts, with the power of untouchable mountains. With impassibility and distant magnitude she meets the measured tread and calibrated gaze of the settlers. But they find not order or even Wordsworthian sublimity, but sudden and absolute violence, metamorphosis of human into animal, a white absence and an emptiness that haunt to dementia the questing, map-making eye of the civilizer.

In her volume of poems *The Journals of Susanna Moodie*, Margaret Atwood renders incidents from the actual records of an early Canadian woman settler. Many of these poems juxtapose the abstracting gaze of the settler with the oblivion and ominousness of the surrounding wilderness. "The Wereman" envisions unacknowledged psychic transformations that such a tension finally brings about:

> My husband walks in the frosted field
> an X, a concept
> defined against a blank;
> he swerves, enters the forest
> and is blotted out.
>
> Upheld by my sight
> what does he change into
> and what other shape
> blends with the under-
> growth, wavers across the pools

is camouflaged from the listening
swamp animals

At noon he will
return; or it may be
only my idea of him
I will find returning
with him hiding behind it.

He may change me also
with the fox eye, the owl
eye, the eightfold
eye of the spider

I can't think
what he will see
when he opens the door.

The husband is a knowable quantity (an "X") only so long as he is
"upheld by my sight." But the abstraction and rationality of the eye
secures only a fragile identity to both husband and wife, conjuring the
possibility of a surreal reversal of vision, the human viewed with the
eye of the alien/animal.

Another poem, "Departure from the Bush," describes this metamorphosis in more benign terms:

I, who had been erased
by fire, was crept in
upon by green
        (how
lucid a season)

first one
 by one, stealthily
(their habitual traces
burnt); then

having marked new boundaries
returning, more
confident, year
by year, two
by two

but restless: I was not ready
altogether to be moved into

They could tell I was
too heavy: I might capsize;

I was frightened
by their eyes (green or
amber) glowing out from inside me

I was not completed; at night
I could not see without lanterns.

He wrote, We are leaving. I said
I have no clothes
left I can wear

The snow came. The sleigh was a relief;
its track lengthened behind,
pushing me towards the city

and rounding the first hill, I was
(instantaneous)
unlived in: they had gone.

There was something they almost taught me
I came away not having learned.

This poem does not render the habitation of the wild by the civilized, but the reverse—the human body inhabited like an ark by the

uncanny creatures beyond rational, civilized boundaries, and by the unbearably lucid but obliterating green and white of the wilderness. Susanna Moody finally returns with relief to the civilized tracks, at which line the traces of the animals disappear.

The "green country" for Atwood does not belong to a sentimental or nostalgic Mother Nature. This mapless, pathless territory is, paradoxically, the psychic underworld, like that described by James Hillman, where the perspective of soul is possible. Another of Atwood's poems, "Procedures for Underground," describes this uncanny dimension: "The country beneath / the earth has a green sun / and the rivers flow backwards; // the trees and rocks are the same / as they are here, but shifted. / Those who live there are hungry; // from them you can learn / wisdom and great power, / if you can descend and return safely." The wilderness is Hades: within a world governed by the hostility of the rational gaze, Artemisian wilderness has gone underground—into the realm of soul.

One last set of contemporary images suggests this realm of soul in rendering the mystery of Artemisian virginity. Eudora Welty in the short story "Moon Lake" shows us a group of young girls at a summer camp. Unlike Artemis' companions they do not sing and dance gracefully to the lyre, but to the hoarse song of Mrs. Gruenwald, "Good morning, Mr. Dip, Dip, Dip, with your water just as cold as ice." The circular lake itself, at night illumined by moonlight, is like the famous Lake Nemi in Italy, the Mirror of Artemis, described in the opening of Sir James Frazer's *The Golden Bough*. And there is in this story a Lady of the Lake, a young girl who carries the depth of the Artemisian, and who, it seems almost fatally, is initiated into the mysteries of the cold, deathly lake. Eventually she falls into the water, and is violently revived—in gestures very much like rape—by the reigning boy scout, Loch Morrison.

This young girl is an outsider, an orphan calling herself Easter (though spelled Esther—Ishtar). She is self-possessed, even self-named, remote and still. And through the eyes of Nina, who recognizes Easter's power while caught in her own meager conventionality, we come to see her distinction: "Easter was the dominant one among the orphans ... [she] was dominant for what she was in herself—for the way she held still, sometimes." Easter, at home in the woods, leads the pack of wild orphans, while Nina and Jinny Love, two *normal* girls, ride longingly in her wake, exploring the brambles and shadows, the hidden parts of the lake, playing dangerous games with Easter's knife. Easter neither accepts nor denies their companionship, and her whole attitude—distant, not caring what others think of her—suggests for the girls a tantalizing freedom and impersonality. Nina senses this quality in Easter's eyes:

> Easter's eyes, lifting up, were neither brown nor green nor cat; they had something of metal, flat ancient metal, so that you could not see into them. Nina's grandfather had possessed a box of coins from Greece and Rome. Easter's eyes could have come from Greece or Rome that day.... The color in Easter's eyes could have been found somewhere, away—away, under lost leaves—strange as the painted color of the ants. Instead of round black holes in the center of the eyes, there might have been women's heads, ancient.

Nina's memory is stirred, sensing that Easter belongs in another country, somewhere ancient, away, under lost leaves. The image of ancient heads of women mirrored in her eyes suggests Nina's recognition of Easter's austere inwardness, linked to something beyond her own life.

Despite her self-possession, however, Easter is fully open to the moment, unconstrained in accepting the intimate fate that waits for her. At night, by the lake glistening in moonlight, Nina watches Easter sleep:

> The pondering night stood rude at the tent door.... Long armed, or long-winged, he stood in the center there where the pole went up. Nina lay back, drawn quietly from him. But the night knew about Easter. All about her.... Easter's hand hung down, opened outward. Come here, night, Easter might say, tender to a giant, to such a dark thing. And the night, obedient and graceful, would kneel to her.

But when Nina tries to imitate Easter's opened hand, she finds no welcome or peace. She falls asleep, dreaming that "her hand was helpless to the tearing teeth of wild beasts." The night is full of wilderness that only its initiate can know. Then, fatefully, Easter falls into the lake, becoming a token to the girls of the hidden portent of this place: "'Moon Lakes are all over the world.'... And into each fell a girl, they dared, now, to think."

Moon Lake, despite the trivial and banal girls' camp on its shore, is really the remaining wilderness—the territory of dreams—ancient, cold, deathly, exquisite, and beautiful, but treacherous. Welty's story suggests the continual accessibility of this territory of the soul, which, while breath-stopping in its purity and delicacy, is also forbidding, fearful—*semnos*. Hippolytus doesn't see the danger, the tearing teeth of wild beasts, that comes from self-conscious imitation of the wild and free. Artemisian virginity, always accessible as a terrain of the soul, instructs us in our shyness, in a certain retrievable grace, and a certain austerity and simplicity of view that come from belonging to oneself. But she instructs us in the violence at the boundary between civilized and wild, and instructs us, we need to remember too, in the ruthlessness needed to navigate the wild and pathless territory.

APOLLO

FREDERICK TURNER

We need a little invocation. So let us actually call the brilliance of the light of the Sun, of Phoibos, of the Shining One, of Reason and Illumination and Inspiration, into this room.[†]

And I especially need that brilliance. When I received this assignment, I felt considerable unease. Apollo is a beautiful god; but in a way a very difficult god for us right now. Our culture has questioned, and in some ways questioned rightly, everything that Apollo stands for. The splendor of his strong, young maleness—the way that in the Kouros sculptures he carries his shoulders as if they weigh nothing—seems too confident for our skeptical age. In Delphi or Olympia I have seen one great frieze in which there's a battle going on all around him, and he stands with one arm raised, and the other pointing, and he's stilling the whole conflict into stone, and his arms seem to weigh nothing. There seems to be a tremendous lightness and strength and certainty about him. But our culture finds that boring, finds that problematic, and for good reason. His brilliance, his clarity, his unity, his association with the Sun, his capacity for order and for a certain domination; the classical forms of the arts with which he's associated—the lyre, the strict order of the lyre, the nomos of the lyre—his urbanity, his idealism, his excellence; all these give us pause. He's not interestingly crippled or doubting or cynical or weak. He's absolutely strong. He is identified with reason, the power of reason, and with the Paean, the hymn of Victory. We find ourselves dazzled by his light.

Consider the stories and myths about him. He is the one who deposed and displaced Rhea and Gaia, the cthonian Earth Goddesses who were the original possessors of Delphi. He replaced them and

---

[†]This contribution was delivered orally, almost without notes. The transcript has been lightly edited for comprehensibility. We have attempted to catch the spontaneity of the occasion by leaving its oral features intact.

became the resident deity at Delphi. He slew Python, the great female dragon that guarded Delphi. He sang the Paean to celebrate his victory and commemorate the conquest of the vale of Tempe in Thessaly, whose original inhabitants worshipped Delphoinae, a blood Goddess, a Goddess of blood sacrifice. He pursued Daphne, of course against her will, and he slew his beloved Hyacinthus, by mistake, with a discus.

We in the twentieth century are very worried by the ways in which heroic reason can clumsily destroy the things that it pursues. As the heirs of Romanticism, of Modernism, and of Post-Structuralism, we prefer the mysteries, and in many ways rightly. We are more interested in the female, the darkness, the disordered and the disseminated, the fragmented, (read the French feminists), the unconstrained, the marginal, the transgressive and anti-traditional, the natural, the unreasoned; the mental and emotional states of the defeated, the oppressed, the underground man. We deplore the mythic overthrow of the ancient matriarchy. We worry about the casting out of Rhea and Gaia from Delphi. So what am I going to say about Apollo? If I said the wrong thing, particularly being a poet and thus a follower of Orpheus the son of Apollo, mightn't I get torn to pieces by Maenads? Mightn't my head float down the Trinity River still singing? And what would happen to my lyre, in these days when nobody knows about poetic meter any more?

But in the context of the other Olympians, I gather up my courage. The genius of polytheism, the tragic joy of polytheism, is that there is a god for every aspect of reality, however contradictory. A monotheistic god must be either peaceful or dynamic, either male or female, either rational or irrational. The Greek gods were all of those. In the context of Athena (who is a female wisdom to go with Apollo's reason), in the context of Artemis's inviolability so poetically evoked, in the context of Hermes the trickster who deconstructs all meaning, perhaps I can speak for and invoke Apollo guarded by that very variety.

We need, I think, beyond that first description of Apollo that I gave, to notice certain strange things about him which might not entirely go with that portrait. I don't want to negate the portrait but to point out a certain depth, certain complexities about it. He is still Apollo the *Phoibos*, the Brilliant One, the Shining One. But there are some other aspects to him. Consider his pursuit of Daphne. He is singing his paean of victory over Python, he has taken over the place of the Oracle, he has brought the light into the darkness, and at that moment as he boasts of his bow, his weapon, the most perfect weapon of all, Eros overhears him and nicks him with one of his own arrows. At that moment he sees the nymph Daphne, and he is consumed with desire for her and pursues her. But she will have nothing of it. She doesn't want him. She doesn't want Apollo! How could any female not want Apollo? But he chases after her, he won't hear the word "no." He's like the scientist who will not hear the word "no" when he is confronted with the mysteries of Nature. But in pursuing Daphne he is like any great prince or hero of reason, in danger of destroying what he loves and reducing the mystery to just another conquest.

We worry now about whether our biogenetic science might reduce the mystery of life to just another conquest. Or our cognitive science might reduce the mystery of mind, of consciousness, to just another conquest. Or that disillusioned by space science, we will no longer be able to look at the heavenly bodies with the same mystical feeling.

But what happens? Apollo, because he's a god, does in fact manage to catch Daphne. He grabs her, he gets hold of her. What happens? Her mystery doesn't disappear, she doesn't shrivel up, she doesn't die. A great miracle happens. Perhaps he has persuaded her in a strange sort of way. Apollo is blessed with something that is beyond mere conquest. Daphne's limbs begin to be covered over by bark, and her fingers elongate and turn into branches and twigs and leaves. She becomes the laurel tree. Now the leaf of the laurel tree, the bay leaf, was, it was said, used by the Oracle at Delphi as a drug to stimulate the power of prophecy. So there's something strange and interesting about that laurel tree into which she turns.

And what does Apollo do? Well, he doesn't chop down the tree, as a Greek God would, I think, be rather expected to. You know, would get angry, and say "Damn you, I'll cut you down." In fact, a much kinder God than any Greek god did something really terrible to a fig tree merely for not giving him some fruit. So what does he do? He adopts the laurel as his tree, he adopts the laurel crown as his own headgear, he makes Daphne the nymph into a sort of symbol or sign of himself. Strange how similar, in some ways, Daphne is to Artemis his sister, how wonderfully dialectical, how wonderfully Greek that they're brother and sister.

Thus we can read this as a sort of allegory of the great mystery of reason. This reason is the true reason science, philosophy, thought, knowledge, analysis must pursue; and it seeks the most mysterious truths. Reason is a god who cannot do anything else. And those truths vanish if they're caught, but they're transformed and become, as transformed, both a trophy and a reminder of failure for the god, a reminder which is also an honor. In the story of Sir Gawain and the Green Knight, the green knight doesn't chop Gawain's head off, but just grazes his neck; and the green girdle, which was the sign of Gawain's failure, then becomes the sign of his honor, and is adopted as the knightly order of the garter. Thus in England they still celebrate the ambiguous success of Sir Gawain.

This pattern is repeated in the wresting of Delphi from the mother goddesses by Apollo, and his defeat of the dragon, an even more ancient female force which they control. He keeps the Pythian oracle, the female oracle, and names his own games after the dragon Python: the Pythian Games. You might draw the conclusion that his pursuit of Daphne, coming just after his defeat of Python, is a kind of gloss on it, a sort of explanation of it.

We could say something like this: dragon slaying is the essential human act we must perform in order to be human, and what the dragon represents is the original and essential malignity of the earliest gods. It's the most terrible, most unthinkable possibility, which is not just that the gods aren't kind or are indifferent, but that they are actually against us—malignant and hostile to human purposes. Imagine it—that God is against us. That is the dragon we must kill. Apollo is the god in us who can kill this dragon, but he then names the games after Python and keeps the Pythian oracle. Likewise the myth of Apollo's killing of Hyacinthus with the discus became the origin of the Hyacinthia, the Hyacinthian ritual which celebrated Apollo. Hyacinthus was stellified by Apollo, turned into a star, his body became a flower, became the hyacinth. Again, the destructive domination of Apollo results not only in the devastation or loss of that which he pursues, but also in a miraculous transformation, a transformation into mystery, an ambiguous oracle. But then that ambiguity is in turn changed by the Delphic priests into hexameter, hexameters measured by the music of the lyre, music that guides the future. The malignity of the gods, you might say, is incorporated into the civilized religion.

And another thing about Apollo that makes him perhaps more complex than you might think at first is that he is, as I said, the father of both Asclepius the healer and Orpheus the poet. You might even take the descent of Orpheus into the underworld—his unsuccessful attempt to bring Eurydice back, his failure, even, as I mentioned before, his being torn to pieces by the Maenads—as being part of the same story. Consider the stellification of his lyre and the strange account of his severed head washing down the river Hebrus to the island at Lesbos, which then becomes the place of poets. Perhaps the greatest poet of all was from Lesbos: Sappho. And in a sense all of that is a kind of gloss upon the nature of Apollo.

Perhaps the meaning of Apollo is the transformation of technique into mystery—or, let me put it this way, it's the tragedy of reason. We can see it perhaps in the history of science, in the history of politics, our pursuit since the Renaissance of a deterministic, linear, mechanistic explanation of the physical world. Our attempts to catch the Daphne of nature by means of the reason of calculus was of course going to fail, but in the process it gave us a great mystery, and the great mystery was a transformation of mathematics into a whole new kind of mathematics and whole new physics that we are entering into now—the non-deterministic, non-linear, evolutionary, creative, unpredictable mathematics that we are getting into: the bay tree, the laurel tree, you might say. In brain science and cognitive science, the Freudian or behaviorist determinism is turning over into a strange new model of the mind, in which there is bottom-up causality and also top-down causality, so that the higher levels of the brain cause its lower levels, and at the same time the lower levels of it cause the higher levels of it. There is a new conception of artificial intelligence, in which what we do is build a chaotic process into an artificial neural network. Again, consider the wonderful transformation that's going on now in our sexual politics. We began, perhaps, in the ancient world, with a patriarchy and a matriarchy that shared the dominion of human life. Then came the age of heroes, in which young males overthrew the old male patriarchs and took charge of the matriarchs. Now what we're seeing is a new age of heroes, and these are the young female heroes who are beginning to find out their own destiny, to move towards places where they can, like Zeus, be first the young rebels but then take over the responsibility of running things.

If we pursue with reason the great mysteries they will yield themselves to us, and in that moment they will dissolve, lose their shape, and become transformed into a greater mystery. The Western scientific democracy of the Enlightenment, of the U.S. Constitution, is the paean of Apollo over Python. But that democracy, at the moment of its triumph, saw Daphne, the effervescent, evanescent, fascinating, unruled wildness of personal being, pursued it, and was defeated. But that personal being, the laurel of that personal being, becomes our tree.

For me, as a poet, Apollo challenges me to make poetry whose metaphors are not merely charming, sensory resemblances, but beautiful, deep, true, scientific laws. And what Apollo tells me is that if I try to do that, I will fail. And in the process of that failure a great mystery occurs, a miracle will happen. And I have to have faith in that, that I must play my lyre, my magic flute down into the underworld and try unsuccessfully to bring Eurydice back.

Let me conclude with a poem by one of the great Orpheuses of our time, Miklós Radnóti, a Hungarian poet who was murdered by the Nazis in 1944. He especially loved Orpheus and Apollo: if you can imagine, he was to poetic meter, what Mozart was to music. As he descended into the hell of the holocaust, a Jewish slave laborer under the Nazis, his poetry became more and more beautiful and Apollonian and perfect and formal and metrical. He fought Hitler with his hexameter. And in translating him, my colleague Zsuzsanna Ozsvath and I feel that we ourselves have had to go down into the underworld to lead him back out and into English.

I read this poem because I think it's the poem of Apollo in our time. He's in a concentration camp. He's writing this poem to his wife Fanni. It's called the "Seventh Eclogue," the seventh of nine eclogues, one of which is lost. This poem was found in a notebook in his pocket when he was dug up from his mass grave, and I've held that notebook in my hand. It's written in pencil, and the notebook is discolored by his bodily fluids. But it's come back out of the grave. It's written in a very beautiful Hungarian meter, a dactylic/trochaic pentameter, which we have rendered into the same meter in English.

Let me explain that Hungarian has beautiful little accents over many of the vowels. He's writing in the dark, he can't even see where to put the accents, and he's just fingering his way over the poem.

THE SEVENTH ECLOGUE

Dusk; and the barracks, the oak stockade with its hem
of cruel wire, they are floating—see! they melt in the night.
The faltering gaze unlocks our frame of captivity
and only the brain can measure the twist of the wire.
But see too, my love, only thus may the fantasy free itself:
dream the redeemer dissolves the wreck of the body,
and off they go homeward, the whole campful of prisoners.

Snoring they fly, the poor captives, ragged and bald,
from the blind crest of Serbia to the hidden heartland of home!
The hidden heartland—O home, O can it still be?
with the bombing? and is it as then when they marched us away?
and shall those who moan on my left and my right return?
Say, is there a country where someone still knows the hexameter?

As thus in darkness I feel my way over the poem,
shorn of its crown of accents, even so do I live,
blind, like an inchworm, spanning my hand on the paper;
flashlight, book, the lager guards took away everything,
and the mail doesn't come, and fog descends on the barracks.
Amid rumors and pests live the Frenchman, the Pole, loud Italian,
the Serbian outcast, the musing Jew in the mountains:
one life in all of these tattered and feverish bodies,
waiting for news, for a lovely womanly word,
for freedom—for an end how dark soever—for a miracle.

On boards among vermin I lie, a beast in a cage;
while the flies' armies rest, the fleas renew the assault.
It's night. Confinement's another day shorter, my love;
life, also, is less by a day. The camp is asleep.
The moonlight rekindles the landscape, retightens the wire;
you can watch through the window the shadows of guards with guns,
pacing, cast on the wall in the many voices of night.

The camp is asleep. See their dreams rustle, my love;
he who startled up snores, turns in his narrow confinement,
falls asleep again, face in a shine. Alone, awake,
I sit with the taste of a cigarette-end in my mouth
instead of your kiss, and the melting dream doesn't come, for
I neither can die nor live any more without you.

Lager Heidenau: in the mountains above Zagubica. July 1944

And that, I think, is what comes to us out of the chaos and the darkness of our century; and its brave commitment to both form and love, reason and feeling, comes to us as a promise, I think, of the next.

HEPHAISTOS

LYLE NOVINSKI

The common idea of the artist as an outsider, remote from the congeniality of the group, maimed prior to creating beauty from inner resources, is fathomable to us in its connection with the archetypal myth of Hephaistos, that artist/maker of the ancient Greek world.

Vincent Van Gogh, a failed artist who cut off his ear, was endeared in film and romance as one who was set apart in life. "Starry, starry night, eventually you were too good to stay, and so you left us," goes the present-day song, recording for us in unwinged verse a universal empathy for an artist who has failed to win public recognition. This failure would be compelling had it remained simply that—a pile of paintings gathered in fews in the museums of the world, testimony that the cache in Amsterdam and Otterloo, where most of them are, would forever state his failure, except for the few very perspicacious collectors who knew differently. Such failure was not to be. Success has finally come, that severed ear story contributing to the obscenity of the millions of dollars now commanded by his paintings. The idea of the artist who is a failure within his lifetime has great currency in popular thought, and, in the case of Van Gogh, is made more potent by the vast sums now needed to purchase his works. Legends of artists abound, telling of tragic ends of shortened lives, rejection of works commissioned, and works never built. All easily support the idea of the artist's typical, existential separation from ordinary life.

In like manner in the shade-sheltered gloom of the Rothko Chapel in Houston, Mark Rothko paintings, stretched anew onto deep stretchers, glow in the deep light—variations on dark chocolate, blood black purples and in some lights balanced by cooler purples. Facing the quartered earth in four ways, the paintings are gathered with an intention of marking a sacred place, sacred to the unknown, and to the known end of an artist in his late life's despair and death. It is curious that brightly sunlit Houston, with its unzoned precincts, has become a special place for the artist's testament, manifest to a sacred priesthood of collectors and educators, and answering our need to find meaning in the work of mystery made by one taking his place in the most powerful mythology of the fifties and the sixties, the pantheon of Abstract Expressionism.

These image-pictures of two artists, one in the early and one in the later part of our century, set apart in kind and in being, easily attract our empathy. They lead us to consider similar elements in the archetype of the craftsman, the god Hephaistos.

Where did we first encounter the inverted power of the lamed god Hephaistos? As the maker of the shield of Achilles before Troy, recalled in Homer's verse as a kind of fabrication unknown to Homer's time but recorded within the verse of the *Iliad* as a possible accoutrement to the heroic saga of war and vengeance and of the nobility of the Mycenaen lords. We again encounter him in Athens, seat of the wondrous production of the fifth century, in ways that link him to the founding myths of Athenian greatness and to the technical marvels of production unearthed from the graves and tombs of earlier centuries. One goes to Athens to see at first hand wonders of the fifth century in that combination of production, guided by the techné of the artist and the ideas that these artifacts engender within the scholar and the casual tourist. There is wonder at the delicacy of the work in marble and the splendor of the work in gold.

At the corner of the Agora, in the shadow of the tall temple to Hephaistos on the high ground, workers live, work, and market in stalls of great variety. This area is now separated by the Piraeus railway from the ancient quarter of craftsmen, welders, bronze casters. The Agora Museum holds the shards, castings, and foundry fragments from this quarter, uncovered by the railroad's severing slice through the border of the Agora. This is the place of Hephaistos, his temple, his hill, his quarter.

It is interesting that a precinct of such complexity should be dedicated to Hephaistos at this time, unless the site of the god also represents a kind of knowing, exposed and made accessible. What aspects of the god reveal themselves here? There are few references in vase painting to the lamed foot of Hephaistos. It is usually absent. In a popular depiction of the revels guiding the return of Hephaistos to Olympos, the club foot does not appear. Hephaistos is identified by his tools, but not by his lameness. In an age in which the marvels of technical proficiency had become commonplace, woundedness is not at the center of discussion. Thus to install the wounded one, the lamed one, as a principal author of the perfection of the Acropolis precinct is especially curious. For the gift of this Athenian achievement is complex, and the presentation perfect beyond measure. One recalls the subtleties of adjustment in the construction of buildings, so that linear measure will not alone be the proof of perfection, but visual perception as well an element in understanding the building. Simple cataloguing of the programmatic content of the Parthenon does not define its quality. Perception is also needed; the insight and intuition of the viewer are implied by the maker. To return to the lamed one, though, as author of this place, is to remind us that this time of complex perfection is also that of the Sophoclean tragedies, wherein the action, the flaw, sets in motion divine retribution in case after case. Each element of character in action is a part of one knowing whole.

The incredible perfection of the Parthenon, containing such a complex program of interrelated stories and carrying so many levels of patriotic and pious meaning that illuminate the initiate skeptic, reveals the position of Hephaistos in Athens. This program teaches that here, in Athens, we understand how knowledge must become Wisdom, through techné, through work, through the arts, through that ability to make imaged that which we know. That this god-like idea of Wisdom is inhabited by men is made clear in the program, which is filled with the understanding of man and what he knows.

The place of the artist, the imaging power of man, is shown on the shield of Athena, surely recalling in its story-telling power that other creation, the shield of Achilles. There were two reliefs on this shield—one, tradition tells us, bearing the portraits of Pericles as Theseus and the other of Phidias as Daedalus, one inhabiting the top half of the shield and the other the lower. The heroes are shown battling the Amazons of the East, reminding the viewer of the connection with the west metopes, where the Amazon battle occurs, and also recalling for the contemporary viewer the recent war with the Persians who came from the East, the sight line of the West metopes. These are things which men knew and which were woven into the complex program of the Parthenon for instruction. Leveled and layered knowing, and the ability to secure connections between layers of knowing, is what is called Wisdom. The complexity of the Parthenon does not serve the purpose of intellectual concealment but of revelation, to supply within the viewer the material and the pattern of wisdom sought and given within works of man, within arts, techné wrought by the lamed one.

Inside the Parthenon, the ancient viewer would have looked at eye level at the sandals of Athena. Worked in gold along their edges, one could observe the battle of the Lapiths and Centaurs. Our Parthenon visitor would recall, on looking at those sandals, that the same story was outside and lower down in the city. At the corner of the Agora it would appear within the western pediment of the temple of Hephaistos. There was in Greek art no paucity of such stories. Myths abound, and varieties of them texture a continual telling in differing shades of meaning for distinct purposes. And so below the sandals, on the base of the great figure of Athena, appeared another story whose presence made more sober the content enriched upon these marble walls. Pandora appears here, fashioned by Hephaistos upon the order of Zeus, in his anger over man's simplicity and easy temptation by the gods. Pandora's appearance in this sacred place seems strange, but indeed it completes the image of man's offering and its perfection before the gods. Men do here what they can and must to the best of their ability, and still the gods appear to pay no attention.

The great ivory and gold figure of the Athena *Parthenos* was the central cult figure in the new tribute to polytheism of the fifth century B.C. It was a wonder of the world, a timbered structure covered with plates of gold and plaques of ivory for the exposed flesh portions of the figure. A tall, armed figure, with shield, helmet, and spear, she was the defending goddess of the city. Phidias guided the work, the complex of stories on the outside of the building in places where sculpture and relief were appropriate to the tradition and, in a singular departure, a frieze band surrounding the cella, the central enclosure within the surround of the peripheral colonnade of severe Doric columns. We know the story of Athena's birth, how she, the figure of Wisdom, appears fully formed and armed when Hephaistos opens Zeus' head to relieve a headache. This image on the east end of the Parthenon accords to Hephaistos a prominent, central position. It is more appropriate to Athens than elsewhere, where the temple begun on the corner of the Agora below was dedicated to Athena and Hephaistos and where there was already a festival of the two in place.

Returning from this gold and ivory figure to the bright attic sun and traversing the south side, the viewer once more would see the battle of Lapiths and Centaurs replayed along the metopes of the south colonnade. It was a curious ornament on the inside, but out here the story takes on major proportions, as one of four depicted on the metopes: Lapiths and Centaurs on the south, Amazons and Greeks on the west, the Trojan War on the north, and the Gods and the Giants on the east. These four images, connecting the founding of Attica with the Gods in battle and defense of Attica, would be familiar enough. Had the visitor been recently to Olympia, which was likely, this same story would there be seen, the battle of the Lapiths and the Centaurs as the greeting pediment on the temple of Zeus in the sacred *temenos*.

In a more severe style the sculptor at Olympia had conceived a program of sculptural adornment that spaced this battle with that of a local legend on the other end of the temple, the principle entrance end. To approach the temple was to see a battle in progress, directed by the central figure Apollo, who appeared as the Centaurs attacked the wedding party of Perithoos, a friend of prince Theseus, the future king of Athens. The Centaurs were there because they were the instructors of Theseus. On the surface, this is a story of man overcoming his beastly nature. The Centaurs were half man, half beast; they were also remnant figures of the old ways, ways of man attached to the world of nature.

In this transitional time, at the close of the sixth century B.C., this temple to Zeus was built to accommodate the change in the understanding of the old ways by juxtaposing on the alternate ends of the temple the qualities of Apollo and Zeus. Apollo reflected a placement in time of a god of action who appeared at the wedding and directed, or stilled, the combat but certainly was within that action. On the opposite end Zeus stood stock-still, awaiting the outcome of the fatal race of Pelops and Oinemeus. Thus at this transitional point in Greek history, the supreme image of knowing, of Zeus as Knowledge, was secured against Apollo as a figure of divine intervention, placed within an image of a distant remembered time, the time of the primitive Centaurs. The idea here is: Knowledge holds all together. The message is: Zeus knows what men know and is enlarged by what men know. On the edge of the great age and with the Acropolis precinct ahead, it appears that men also know, as the artist suggests, that the gods no longer intervene in our actions.

Astonished at the ancient gold face masks, gold for cups, jewelry, shimmering discs scattered over the body of the Mycenean king, tiny granulated large sand-like particles arranged in arabesques on the rings and brooches in the Athens Museum, I stood still. "Where are the tools?" I thought, looking at a spool of gold wire. "Where are the tools?"—tongs and drawplates, files and vises, and then, the multiple alloys, measured today in carats for our convenience. This ancient glittering world before the Trojan war, stuff of Priam's treasure, was wrought by men who knew and taught their sons the how of wrought things. How, with bronze drills, to fashion drawplates and pliers, how to pull gold, king of ductile metals, through descending holes in bronze plates to reduce it to a thread the size of horsehair. How to affix with the liquid sun of melted amber tiny particles of gold in exquisite patterns on a piece; how to raise the temperature slowly until the burning amber would extract from one molecular layer the base metal of the alloy and fuse the tiny pallions of gold onto the ring or bracelet, buckle, or breastplate. Magic would such a skill appear to be, and power would attach to the wearer of such items. Thus, they would be thought worthy of returning to the earth with the body in death, so that their magic beauty caught in the grave might await our awestruck eyes centuries later.

These artifacts were remembered in Homer, singing the story in a time long distant from Mycenae or Troy, but bearing in the details of that memory the loss of an heroic age, and, along with it, the equal loss of the techné that made its exquisite handiwork possible. Men stand before other men in battle, but a barbarian clearing the way into a village does not know that he may kill the only man in the country who knows how to alloy gold, or forge, or smelt from the earth ore the metals needed. The concept of barbarian to the Greek is about not knowing. Remembering, in the Homeric way, paved the way for the reacquisition of the attendant losses hidden within the loss of the Heroic age. Cattle will breed, wheat will grow, wine will ferment, but art, the wrought surface, is done only with knowledge.

In the economy of skills in an ancient village, warriors and workers in the fields would be the same. Without the strength or agility to compete in field or battle, other skills would serve for some—the blacksmith, forger, artificer of pottery, metals, supplier of goods and ornament. Thus, is the apartness of the artificer by custom or by metaphor? It is said that Hephaistos was the son of Zeus and Hera, and the *Iliad* contains accounts of his being thrown from Olympos on separate occasions by each parent. Zeus was angry over the intervention of Hephaistos in a quarrel between Hera and him. Thetis tells us of Hera's disgust at his deformity. In any case, there is a separation from the parent, or parents, needed for the one who makes, for the artist. Interesting as well, in view of our separation from making and from those who make, is the myth that he may well be the offspring of Hera alone, who conceived him herself. This story may be associated with images of the arts as connected to the feminine, though our images of Hephaistos—as armorer, forger, and fire master—are quite in the masculine mode. The close connection of Hephaistos to his mother points to the fact that the arts themselves have domestic roots. For example, architecture begins with weaving, and our language still recalls the fabric of a building in its description.

It is said that Hephaistos returned to Olympos at the bidding of Dionysus. He had constructed a throne that trapped his mother, but he was persuaded by Dionysus, with much drink, to return and free her. A number of vase paintings depict him as riding a mule led by Dionysus and the revelers. In some cases the revelers and the mule are ithyphalic, and, in one case, the mule's ithyphalic condition supports a krater of wine. The wine is needed for the rites of Dionysus. The mule, and in some cases the accompanying lion, are images of impotence, marking the time as that of one aspect of Dionysus, the winter of things impotent. It is interesting that Hephaistos on his return is part of a Dionysian rite, suggesting the closeness of the arts and celebration. The connection between the ithyphalic power depicted on the libation vessel of Dionysus and the image of the impotent mule of Hephaistos in an ithyphalic state suggests power, or at least purpose, to the bearer. There is an interesting corollary here between power and potency—one has the power to move, as art certainly does, but it is marked with some limits in physical or generative terms. The recognition of the power of Hephaistos' mule and of Hephaistos, for the mule is common to many representations of him, places him necessarily in the fallow time, the winter of events. Does this say that the power of art precedes the potency of summer deeds? Or is it another way of speaking symbolically of the separateness of the artist through the image of the lamed one?

The arts have done before the gods what they can, representing knowledge, fashioning even Wisdom from its factual earthen clods, giving rise to images of great loftiness, as though so bid by Olympos and all of its citizens. In parallel ways the craft has obeyed, as did the craft of Hephaistos, who fashioned chains to execute Zeus' anger at Prometheus, fashioned tethers bidden from outside.

Hephaistos was the separated one, the foreigner. He came as a god of volcanoes and became the god of furnaces, of magic, of the unbelievable. In many ways he is the mysterious other of our experience, the figure who lies behind the knowing of a crafted thing, a worker hidden, surprising, powerful, and lamed. Away from parents, or unevenly parented, he has been cast out, then cared for, and finally invited home in revelry.

Hestia

Mary Vernon

In order to speak of Hestia, the hearth, or of her Roman self, Vesta, let us tell a story. You will see that our story, at first, is not directly about Hestia, the firstborn child of Kronus and his sister Rhea, Hestia, the first victim of child sacrifice to prolong the rule of the father, Hestia the silent, centered, pacific one. Knowing her, I assume she was the *last* child to be regurgitated. She was the only Olympian who did not rebel against Zeus in the famous case of the hundred knots. You may want to see her as we tell the story. She is a banked fire, its heat saved under a covering of white ash and earth. The best size for this sort of fire is about 11 inches high and 15 inches across, as it was at Delphi, where the Olympian conqueror Apollo allowed it to stay, carved in stone. It is the *omphalos*, the mound in the center of the world. In a related gesture, Roman servants of Vesta (Vestal virgins) who lost their virginity while in office, were buried alive, or we might say, overbanked, then dug up and buried with appropriate, patrician honors. Hestia appears in statues as a heavily veiled, mature virgin. An old maid. A family member, we might add, who proves essential over and over again.

The story I wish to tell is told by Ovid, in the *Metamorphosis*, Book Eight, translated into English by John Dryden. Lelex, who tells this story, speaks of two neighboring trees which grew in Phrygia.

> Here Jove with Hermes came; but in disguise
> Of mortal men conceal'd their deities;
> One laid aside his thunder, one his rod;
> And many toilsome steps together trod:
> For harbour at a thousand doors they knock'd,

Not one of all the thousand but was lock'd.
At last an hospitable house they found
A homely shed; the roof, not far from ground,
Was thatch'd with reeds, and straw, together bound.
There Baucis and Philemon liv'd, and there
Had liv'd long marri'd, and a happy pair:

The hospitable old pair are noble in their poverty, remembering virtue
toward one another:

Command was none, where equal love was paid,
Or rather both commanded, both obey'd.

The guests are welcomed and a seat is drawn up for them; before they
sit, cushions stuffed with straw are laid to raise the seat. Then Baucis

rakes the load
Of ashes from the hearth, and spreads abroad
The living coals; and, lest they should expire,
With leaves, and bark she feeds her infant fire:
It smokes; and then with trembling breath she blows,
'Till in a cheerful blaze the flames arose.
With brush-wood, and with chips she strengthens these,
And adds at last the boughs of rotten trees.

Baucis puts the little, burnished kettle on. It shines like gold. Quickly a
hearty peasant dinner is in the works—all the best vegetables and odd
treasured bits of bacon long stored-up. Olives, cornels pickled in the
lees of wine, garden salad, curds and cream, new laid eggs roasted in
the fire, and liquor in an earthen jug embellished with figures; plums,
apples, grapes, and wrinkled dates, dry figs, surrounding a milk-white
honeycomb. The old hosts bathe the feet of the guests in a beechen pail
filled with water gently warmed. From the couple's bed, covered in
the rags which are the best robes of Philemon and Baucis, the guests
dine at a mended table. All is rubbed, oiled, waxed, and clean.

> But the kind hosts their entertainment grace
> With hearty welcome, and an open face:
> In all they did, you might discern with ease,
> A willing mind, and a desire to please.

Then the gods reveal themselves by a miracle—replenishing the bowls of wine with wine of heavenly quality and making the bowls dance:

> Mean-time the beechen bowls went round, and still,
> Though often empty'd, were observed to fill;
> Fill'd without hands, and of their own accord
> Ran without feet, and danc'd about the board.
> Devotion seiz'd the pair, to see the feast
> With wine, and of no common grape, increas'd;
> And up they held their hands, and fell to pray'r,

Now they wanted to sacrifice their only goose; she was their pet and their sentry. They pursue her until she finds sanctuary at the feet of Jove. In short order the goose is saved; the impious district is condemned. Philemon and Baucis are shown as escaping to a mountain height and forbidden to look back; their little hut grows into a temple of marble and gold, and the noble, old pair are offered the granting of their wish—to serve in Jove's temple and, when the time comes, die in the same hour.

The story of Philemon and Baucis strikes me for its long list of Hestiatic virtues. In devotion to Hestia, Philemon and Baucis are hearth-centered, permanently settled (at least until the flood of Jove puts the hut under water), intimate, receptive, and self-sufficient. The banked fire is at the heart of Philemon and Baucis's hut. As the first act of hospitality, Baucis "rakes the load of ashes from the hearth, and spreads abroad the living coals," so that the comforting fire opens up to warm the guests. Hestia is the hearth, and holds the center of the home. She is the center of the city and her spark, from the hearth of the chief, lit all the hearths of the town. Without Hestia, there is no home or town, because a place for living has a fire in its center. Philemon and Baucis, long before Jove and Hermes knocked at the door, sat together at their hearth year after year.

Rude and fragile though it was, the hut of Philemon and Baucis was permanent. Within the walls, which must have been constantly repaired, the hearth would be there, in the same place, all their lives, perhaps all their parents lives; and Philemon and Baucis did not want to be somewhere else. They never lived on the road. They never took a weekend away at the Hyatt Regency to renew their relationship. It was already permanent around the hearth.

Philemon and Baucis were intimate. Inside the hut, the family was complete. No one could share completely the things that Philemon and Baucis knew of their hearth and their story. Only by sharing their hearth permanently could we share in that family. Intimacy is guarded by the tending of a single fire. To join their family, you would need to leave your fire, and your fire would go out. Unless you married into their family and brought a coal from your hearth with you, there would be no way to stay with them long without losing your place. You might think you could leave your servant to tend your fire and live with Philemon and Baucis for a while. But the fire belongs to the tender. You would be without a hearth of your own. It is Jove and Hermes who are taking a risk here, being the guests.

A guest is vulnerable, in need of a comforting fire on a dark and stormy night. The rules of Hestia demand hospitality in receiving guests. So it is a great test that the two gods devise for the district of Phrygia: to travel as wanderers and to take a measure of the hospitality of the region. As we know, everybody failed the test except Philemon and Baucis, who gave comfort to strangers and opened their carefully banked hearth and meager pantry for them. The wages of failure in hospitality are usually pursued by the Furies; in this case it was an inundation, as in Genesis or Gilgamesh. This may be the new, patriarchal sort of sentencing. Instead of punishing only the guilty, as the Fates would have done, Philemon and Baucis get flooded too. Then Jove and Hermes pay them back with a temple house in which they may keep the hearth, and Hestia has to start all over again. Just as the hearth of home is commanded to protect the guest, the town hall (which, as Pindar says, is Hestia's portion of the city) is to comfort and protect suppliants from harm. I presume the punishment of Furies awaits the town hall which fails in this. To be receptive is a command.

But to be self-sufficient is a virtue of Hestia as well. Without a long time of storing-up, Philemon and Baucis could not have served the olives and the eggs, the curds and cream, the figs and honeycomb. Hestia, in one of her aspects, is called Hestia of the reserves—the pantry Hestia of whom the Greeks spoke when they said "we must sacrifice to Hestia" and meant "Charity begins at home." My aunt used to admonish her family, when guests were at the table: "FHB!" I suppose she thought none of the guests knew it meant: Family, hold back!" The same aunt used to say to the guests: "You may have as little as you like," a statement well outside the rules of Hestia or Baucis. Philemon and Baucis had to save the bit of bacon in the rafters, to get by, to make do, to scrimp—dinners take forethought. To have things put by for the future is another rule of the hearth. The banking of the fire and the veiling of Hestia is the saving, the reserves. The fire is held intimately, but it is also stored up. Hestia is saving herself for something. The town hall, which must give sanctuary to the suppliant, must have something to give, socked away by prudent management. The hearth in us that cares for visiting ideas and images must have a storehouse to feed them with. When gods come calling as if they were commoners, the pantry must be as full as our poverty allows.

The reason I have told the story of Philemon and Baucis is that it is redolent with the lessons of Hestia. Her fire, which only grows more bright by being seen as a metaphorical fire, burns at the center of any real home, and at the center of any living city. At the center of the planet, the fire is not even metaphorical; Earth is a banked fire and a living home. Even if, at the surface, Poseidon's ocean currents and thundering steeds circle incessantly, it is the central fire they spin around. There is a home fire somewhere at the core of all of us.

The house of Philemon and Baucis seems to me to be in the style of the first houses. Hestia is credited with the invention of domestic architecture. Her temples in Rome (where she was Vesta) are round, built in the shape of neolithic huts and ennobled by the cannons of the Greek Tholos, the round temple, which also came from the neolithic hut. I was struck just yesterday by the story of a friend of mine who said his son came to live with him for a month and had made his rectangular guest room into a round room by placing all his earthly possessions in an oval around his futon on the floor. "The room was round then," the father said, "It looked like there should be a little campfire on the futon."

Philemon and Baucis were perfect in their receptivity. Hestia's essence is receptivity, but we should be careful about the meaning of that. The power of her receptivity is clear in everything about her. She is waiting, reserved. She does not move (any stop for her is a stop away from the center). She will always be in the same place; you can find her. So you come home by stepping toward her.

She commands shelter for the guest. But the guest is only a guest, not an intimate. Guest is not family. Where you are an intimate—a creature of earth, a living animal, one who knows the neighborhood, one who has bound himself to a place or an idea, the child of the region, a soul working on itself, a dog in her own bed, you may pass through to the center. Off-world, as they call it in the movie *Bladerunner*, the realm of replicants, is anywhere you have no home fire. In *Bladerunner*, even the replicants want to come home.

Sometimes simple receptivity can be mistaken for intimacy. Not everywhere you are well-received will you pass through to intimacy. There is the odd story of the sieve of Tuccia. Tuccia, a Vestal Virgin of Rome, is accused of the impious loss of her virginity. Since she is dedicated to maintaining the sacred fire of city, she is sworn to remain a virgin. If she is guilty she will be buried alive. Tuccia proved the falsity of the charges by travelling the mile to the Tiber, filling a sieve with water, and walking back to the forum with the sieve still full. She poured it at the feet of the Senators. The sieve, which seemed full of holes, held water. It held the water as the hearth holds a guest. The hearth itself influences who shall pass through to intimacy at any hearth and who shall be simply comforted.

ARES

WILLIAM BURFORD

Ares is the embodiment of rage aimed at the destruction of the enemy, whether one man or a whole army, a rage that possesses the human heart and only abates when the enemy lies dead before us. "Tell me," Sophocles, the tragic dramatist, asks: "Who is the slayer, Who the slain?" Consider Oedipus and Laius at the crossroads, neither giving way, until the young man slays the older, his own father, unrecognized. Or Achilles and Agamemnon in the opening book of the *Iliad* when Achilles draws his sword to kill Agamemnon, but Athena stops him, breaking for a moment the hold of murdering anger over men. Though the gods, for wise reasons, may enter human history and sometimes soften or correct men's rage, the world, if left to itself, would bear out Hegel's view of it: "History is a chopping block." The material for this chopping is men's flesh and bone, and sometimes even the gods' immortal substance, that of Ares himself and his progeny. The death of Kyknos, a son of Ares in the poem "The Shield of Herakles," attributed to Hesiod, is described like an autopsy of body parts.

> Herakles the powerful, swiftly
> struck, and forcibly with the long spear,
> between helm
> and shield, where the throat
> had been left unguarded, beneath
> the chin, and the manslaughtering ash spear
> cut through both tendons

The destruction of the form of the human body, the principal image of the beautiful, gives the world over to ugliness and pain, and, though he is one of the Olympian gods *who live forever*, Ares can be caught in his own destructiveness, can come close to *destructive death*.

> The bitter sorrow closed on Ares,
> and drawing his sharp sword
> he swept in against Herakles
> ...but as he came in
> Amphitryon's son, insatiate
> of the terrible battle-cry,
> stabbed with full force
> into the thigh left bare under
> the elaborate shield, and twisting
> with the spear tore
> a great hole in the flesh
> and beat him to the ground

This hole, this wound that would be fatal to mortals, is closed by Zeus, father of Ares, though Zeus will say that of all the gods he scorns only Ares for being a stirrer of strife. Yet Ares, however denounced, has his place, his role among both gods and men. He is the instigator of intoxicating combat and deadly sadness.

> So they fought on in the likeness of fire
> fought in the bright air, with the sun's
> sharp glitter

Old Priam, King of Troy, mourning his dead sons, uses words that are barer: "All these Ares has killed."

Much later in time we hear this grieving tone in the refrain of a poem by Yeats, "Easter 1916," commemorating the Irishmen killed in the uprising of that year against the English. Yeats says, "A terrible beauty is born."

Throughout the *Iliad* this union of beauty and destruction recurs—in the leaf-headed spears, an often repeated epithet, a kind of motif, in the poem. But the beauty of deadly weapons does nothing to change their deadliness. Still, "the day without pity," as the day of a

---

man's death is called, is brought by the spear head. Without this day we would not have the particular kind of poetic beauty, of sharp sorrow that marks the tone of the *Iliad*. That Ares is uncaring is the hard background to the human action.

There is a sixteenth century German woodcut with the caption "War, the Father of All Things" which at first seems an extravagant claim, but is borne out by what our wars reveal about our nature. One of these things is an increase in the intensity of compassion between men, of comradely love and the gestures of love that men do not allow themselves in ordinary daily life. Even Achilles, the most efficient of war machines in his pitilessness, is moved by pity for the prostrate, aged Priam embracing his knees, who has come to beg for his son Hector's body. Achilles lifts Priam up in a gesture that can be seen again in other wars, in, for example, the great painting by Velazquez, *the Surrender of Breda*, in which the victorious Spanish commander moves to embrace his defeated Dutch opponent with fraternal graciousness. Ares would have had them fight on to extinction. Or does the god suspend his ruthlessness briefly so that this deeply civilized moment at the end of a war can take place? Does Ares or another god demand it?

When, in the *Homeric Hymns* to the gods, we read the Hymn dedicated to Ares, we are at first astonished to discover that the god depicted in the Hymn is a radically different one from the god of war we expected. We now face the other side of the coin, a god of peace, or so the young warrior addressing him, praying to him, assumes that he is, and thus invoked will help the youth escape a violent death. But at the same time the hero must avoid cowardice; gentleness must be mixed with courage; and this new Ares, as it were, and his suppliant must walk together a delicate balance between martial power and peaceful mildness.

> Ares has armour of bronze
> Ares has powerful arms....
> Hear me,
> Helper of mankind,

dispenser of youth's sweet courage
beam down from up there
your gentle light
on our lives

Now he is called: Helper of Mankind with "gentle light" to beam
down on our lives." We are in an entirely different psychological
world here from that of the violent energy of the destroying god. But
desirable as gentleness is, to surrender to it, Old Ares warns us, brings
a loss of energy. Ezra Pound, in one of his early troubadour poems,
has Bertrans de Born cry out:

Damn it all! all this our South stinks peace.
. . . .
I have no life save when the swords clash.

This is, of course, extravagant play-acting. The Ares of this bravado is
a parody of the old war god. But all the same, would it not strike a
chord in us coming from a character in a Shakespearean history play?
In any case, nothing could be farther from the serious speaker of the
"Hymn to Ares," who asks his god of peace to help him resist the
impulse to join the fighting again.

restrain
that shrill voice in my heart
that provokes me.
You, happy god,
give me courage,
let me linger
in the safe laws of peace
and thus escape
from battles with enemies

Courage here means courage not to fight. The pacifist plot of the Hymn,
in which the speaker must choose between violence and peace, has its
echo in Christian thinking. Pagan Ares gives way to a Christian Ares. We

must love our enemies, not kill them. In the history of the god, however, this is not his ultimate role. The modern sensibility brings yet another appearance of Ares. He enters the realm of art.

In 1868 the French painter, Edouard Manet, painted a picture, *Luncheon in the Studio*, which can now be seen in Munich in the Bavarian State Collections. This picture like others in the France of the nineteenth century is a paean to the pleasures of the good life — the pleasure of eating well, what the French call the pleasures of the table, and drinking well, and enjoying a choice cigar, and having coffee served by an assiduous servant, and dressing well, and keeping a little black cat for diversion. The pleasures of the gods. Indeed, the persons in Manet's painting *are* the gods; they have access, it seems, to the immortal food, the ambrosia. Of these three figures the chief one (whom the painting is most about) is a very elegant, almost exotic young man (actually Manet's illegitimate son) who looks slightly above and past us, slightly aloof, in his black velvet jacket and gold boater, entirely assured, as the painting itself is, a proof of the power of style. Among the objects that form the setting for this young dandy, are a saber and an antique helmet with visor, sitting propped against the arm of a sofa. When the painting was first exhibited, the critics complained they could not see why such martial trappings were present in a picture that had nothing to do with war. But the saber and the helmet are not out of place or foreign to the spirit of Manet's picture. He is evoking the ancient theme of the young man and war; and though the figure of his son is not wearing the helmet or wielding the saber, though they have been laid aside for luxurious clothes, still they are there in the painting as an echo of war, of Ares.

However, this substitution of the artificial for the actual, of art for combat, tends to leave the old god no more than a kind of theatrical prop in the repertoire of Manet's studio. The power of painting replaces almost any other. Yet we might remember that only two years after Manet painted *Luncheon in the Studio* the Franco-Prussian War broke out, the Germans were in Paris, old Ares reared his head again.

APHRODITE
AND THE ENSOULED WORLD

JOANNE H. STROUD

> The soul is always an Aphrodite.
> —Plotinus, *Enneads VI*

From Aphrodite, glorious Aphrodite, comes the gift of beauty itself. To awaken desire, to capture and hold our attention in the sensual world, she touches all things, rendering them visible and arresting. Her enchantment bestows brilliance on even the most mundane, and her gifts extend beyond the individual to all living beings. Walter Otto describes her beneficence as "not so much the ecstacy of desire as the charm which kindles and propels it.... Not only men and beasts but plants, inanimate images and appearances, even thoughts and words, derive their winning, moving, overwhelming sweetness from her." Thus we are indebted to her for making us see the world as both beautiful and desirable. When the first space travelers looked back and saw the world's lovely configuration, perhaps we ushered Aphrodite, long diminished, back into our lives.

Mythology holds that Aphrodite emerges with the pearlescent dawn, clothed in hues of pink and aqua, an ephemeral beauty visible for a few radiant moments as darkness lingers at the cusp of the heavens, soon to be eclipsed by the incandescent light of day. She is always on the margin—of day and night, of sea and shore. She is the misty fusion of water and air in the luminescent sea foam or morning dew. The four elements of nature are her domain, with one never exclusively dominant. Even her earthiness partakes of an airy lightness. In gods and humans she quickens pulsations of rapture and the lyric voice. To embrace Aphrodite is to embrace joyous excess.

Aphrodite has many prototypes, among them earlier Mideastern goddesses such as Ishtar, Astarte, and Iannana. Her name is not Greek, and yet she is the most Greek of goddesses. She is the embodiment of fertility, procreation, and prosperity. She is the essence of the life of the senses, and yet she transcends the purely natural world. She is the spirit of beauty in nature. C. G. Jung never let us forget the nature/spirit connection: "Nature is not matter only, she is also spirit. Were that not so, the only source of spirit would be human reason."

Aphrodite's special range of powers emerges from her diverse origins. Two very distinct stories of her birth are recorded in mythological lore, both highly sexually oriented. In Hesiod she is related to the oldest generation of the Olympians. She emerges full-grown from Uranus' genitals, which bobbed in the sea after Kronos castrated his father for the rape of Gaia and for burying their children in the earth. A violent beginning for such a beautiful creature!

Aphrodite is coupled to two sides of the father, the exalted spiritual side, but also to the senex, the seedy, seminal stuff of masculinity. She is his sole creation, reawakening fantasies of youthful energy, puer fantasies. James Hillman explains this rapport between fantasy and disillusionment: "Without Kronos and the senex-despair of the complex, Aphrodite and her illusions might never float in off the foam."

Hesiod relates in the *Theogony* that she came ashore at Cythera and "grass grew up beneath her shapely feet." But Cythera was too small an island for her, and she quickly departed for Cyprus which henceforth she called home. Her companions, whom she is rarely without, play significant ancillary roles. Love (Eros) accompanies her, the great magnet, the motivator; Longing (Himeros) is in her entourage, symbolizing the unslakable thirst that propels one ever onward toward the object of desire.

Her birth as Aphrodite Pandemos in the alternate version is less violent. She has a mother, Dione, an immortal sea nymph, making her less singularly a father's fancy. She is the off-spring by natural means of Zeus, who in the *Iliad*, refers to her as his "dear daughter."

Whichever version we accept, Aphrodite appears as strongly solar, her radiant goldenness a dominant feature. She is persuasive, hard to resist. Paul Friedrich points out the linguistic associations of her goldenness—gold and honey, gold and speech, gold and semen; all are linked symbolically in her appeal. Jean Shinboda Bolen suggests that procreation and verbal creation have a common nexus.

Although not lunar like Artemis, Aphrodite does relate to the rhythms of the tides, and she has astral features as well. As Venus, she is the evening planet appearing first in the twilight sky and nestling near the new moon. As the morning star, she is the last to leave the heavens. Keith Critchlow draws a remarkable pentagonal diagram of the planetary pattern that the planet Venus' pathway takes in the heavens, entering and leaving. Aphrodite is always betwixt and between places, both spatially and emotionally. Her proximity signifies a possible turning, a moment of change, a transformation.

She is the essence of summer, and she favors all manner of fruits, flowers, and fragrances. "She draws forth the hidden promise of life," as Ginette Paris describes it. Her fertile beneficence stimulates the maturation of apples, peaches, and pomegranates. Among flowers she is particularly associated with the rose, but she also likes the daisy and the lily; she is always described as "garlanded." She is a favorite of small animals and birds; swans and doves circle about her and do her bidding. In her presence fierce animals are tame and gambol in the sun in pairs. She is wafted by Zephyr, the west wind, or rides on the dolphin, a pink scallop, or a cockle shell. Botticelli's *Birth of Venus* immortalizes her wispy veiled figure emerging from the sea on an open-faced scallop shell.

From the moment of her appearance she is involved in dressing, undressing, and perfumed bathing. "The Hours received her happily and happily put ambrosial garments around her," the "Hymn to Aphrodite II" records. Her garments possess the power to enchant. In Book 14 of the *Iliad* the goddess Hera, usually at odds with her over the sanctity of marriage vows, borrows a magic girdle from Aphrodite in order to seduce Zeus and to lure him away from the battlefield.

Aphrodite's domain also embraces jewelry, and of course she is lavishly bedecked. The pearl imitates her power to transform ugliness into beauty: irritated by a bit of gritty sand, it emerges from the sea as a luminous gem. In other applications, her beauty and magic are more ephemeral, of the present, of transient sensuality. Clothes illustrate this phenomenon. They are not meant to last forever. Cosmetics, another of her areas, have to be reapplied endlessly.

Among surviving cult statues, those of Aphrodite are more numerous than any other deity. The collections of the Louvre verify this. In classical times she was always portrayed clothed, if only barely, often with a wet, clinging garment but never in a stiff pose. Her body is usually twisting and full of movement. She is perpetually changing, the goddess of turning. She is described as having "sparkling eyes" and a "beautiful backside" (callipge). When Praxiteles fashioned a naked statue of her, fourth century B. C. Athens was shocked. In our time, contemplating a copy of this sculpture known as the *Cnidian Aphrodite*, Kenneth Clark precisely summarizes the eyes of "innocence" that the modern world seems to have lost: "[A]ll who saw her [Aphrodite] felt that the instincts they shared with beasts, they also shared with the gods. It was a triumph for beauty."

As one of the Olympians, Aphrodite had, for the Greek world, supernatural and religious import. Yet, ever since her early prominence, she has raised a conflict; at its crux is whether her distinguishing feature is merely earthly consciousness "exalted to the highest purity" and therefore merely human—or whether sensual beauty has deeper inherent soul or spiritual value. Otto affirms her reach: "Her enchantment brings into being a world where loveliness moves toward delight, and all that is separated desires blissful fusion into oneness. In it all possibilities and desires are included, from dark animal impulse to the yearning for the stars."

Appropriately for one who is an admixture of light and dark, of ocean spray and morning dew, Aphrodite often mediates across the chasm that divides mortals and immortals, perhaps because she is effective in both realms. Her liminality is an important aspect of her crossover identity. The liminal, being on the edge, always challenges the ethical societal norms of the middle and therefore is adjudged perilous. In modern political parlance, she would be labelled an extremist of either right or left because she threatens the comfortable status quo. Either by awakening unrealized desires for aesthetic beauty or by repelling those who value crudeness, she breaks down barriers to create openings for new experiences. Through an eruption of novel attractions, she challenges the entrenched ego.

Aphrodite is the goddess who makes unions possible, whether brief or enduring, even unlikely ones. The complexity of relationships attracts her, and particularly those in triads, whether male or female. She is accompanied by three Graces, the three Hours, or involved with the three Moirai. In one of her guises, as *Urania*, she is deemed the eldest of the Moirai, linking her to the cycle of birth, life, and death.

How can such an alluring, lively creature connect with the pale, shadowy world of the dead? This nexus suggests that wholehearted acceptance of Aphrodite yields knowledge of both life and death. Rejection of Aphrodite implies two shadows: a belittlement of the sensual world or an avoidance of the uncomfortable awareness of life as inherent part of death and death as part of life. Perhaps this explains the animosity she can arouse in those wishing to avoid full-hearted confrontations with both aspects of the living process.

The enmity is perhaps engendered by her attitude toward marriage, with which she is frequently at odds. Having possessed many lovers, she of course encourages love affairs. Yet with each of her own amorous liaisons, a virginal aspect is manifested. In a curious sense, she is a perpetual virgin, meaning she is never permanently attached. As Esther Harding describes this aspect, she is "one in herself," one who does not need another to be complete. She is not the half of any pair. She is never raped, because she is the teacher when it comes to lovemaking. For Aphrodite, the act of love is an art and never hasty, as opposed to Dionysian sex, which is more animalistic, more like a hunger—a compulsive urge, demanding quick gratification.

Aphrodite is a nonconformist, cut from a different mold than any other god or goddess. She takes a lover with no regret, and yet those who serve her are apt to feel helpless, even masochistic. Even in her choice of companions there is paradox. *Ananke* (necessity) and *Aidos* (shame) join her entourage, and in odd ways they belong. Necessity is the core of all complexes, of which she is a great evoker. Shame exhibits itself in everything from a simple blush to extreme humiliation. John Sanford and George Lough examine the language of masochism that connects with the goddess: "For Aphrodite was said to 'ensnare people's hearts,' to inflict people with the 'lashes of longing,' and to 'chain' people with her charms. She herself was often pictured in Greek art as Aphrodite in chains. For hers is the power that binds; she binds the soul to her, people to themselves, lovers to each other." Strangely, masochism serves the feminine. They add: "And all of this compensates in many men an ego development that has gotten too far away from its roots in the world of the feminine."

In exploiting passion and ecstacy Aphrodite can trigger some very uncomfortable combinations. She is the essence of pairing, but frequently the dyad enlarges to become an uneasy love triangle. Allowed to choose her own husband, she picked Hephaistos, even though all could predict that she would never remain faithful to this lame but highly skilled god. Although seemingly unequal, this bonding affirms that beauty and craft have an affinity, a need to enhance one another. We understand the connection if we appreciate that ephemeral, aphroditic beauty can be rendered into manifest, durable form through hephaistian craftsmanship.

In her other major relationship, her long affair with Ares, the attraction is again an association of apparent dissimilarities that are actually confluent. A haunting association exists linguistically between the closeness of *Eros*, Aphrodite's child, with *Eris*, the goddess of strife, and *Ares*, god of war, indicating that beauty and the martial arts are never as remote as we might expect. Her pairing with Hephaistos produced no progeny; yet with Ares came three diverse children—a girl, Harmonia (Harmony), and then in disquieting opposition, two sons, Phobus (Fear) and Deimos (Terror). Even in her affair with

Hermes, who is sometimes called the father of Eros, similarity and difference reflect the powers she repeatedly draws to herself.

Her volatile nature bears more kinship to Hermes than to most other Olympians. Both are forever changing, unpredictable, always unreliable. Both lie, both steal, and both like to laugh when caught in delinquencies. The offspring of this union is an hermaphrodite, sharing equally in both of their names and both sexual natures. In alchemical literature, Aphrodite by herself, as Venus, has an androgynous nature, containing both masculine and feminine energies.

Aphrodite has Eros as both companion and son. Sometimes she is vying for his attention; sometimes she is sending him on missions that further her causes. This bond exemplifies the problem confronting the young son who struggles to release himself from erotic attachment to the mother, or the older woman hungering for a handsome youth. In the personal realm the closeness of the tie between Aphrodite and Eros is apparent: "She is the active principle of Eros which enables us to be related to our own emotions, and also to touch the emotional substance of another," Nancy Qualls-Corbett explains. Relationships under her aegis are so intense that even the Olympians had difficulty extricating themselves from emotional attachments under her governance.

Aphrodite herself cannot always escape the complex emotions she arouses in others. Occasionally she is ensnared in a painful affair of the heart. Her relationship to Adonis is post-Homeric but illustrative of the love of the mature woman for a youthful man. Here she is forced to share Adonis with Persephone for part of the year. Priapus, the vulgar manifestation of sexual urges, is the son of Aphrodite by either Dionysus, Hermes, or Adonis. Ultimately, she abandons him, perhaps because his nature is too compulsively sexual for her more refined taste.

Beyond her involvements with the deities of the pantheon, Aphrodite has a propensity for human relationships. Some say that Zeus, envious of her power over immortals (except Artemis, Athena, and Hestia) and wanting to pay her back for her provocations, caused her passions to be aroused by the human herdsman, Anchises. The

"Hymn to Aphrodite I" describes this fateful encounter: "And when she saw / him, Aphrodite, lover of laughter, she / loved him, and a terrifying desire seized her heart." Aphrodite is not the guardian of longevity. Often those rapturous interludes she stimulates quickly evanesce. Instead of leaving Anchises after a brief affair, she remains bound to him, and this union produces her favorite child, Aeneas.

When summoned by mortals, Aphrodite often responds. The tenth book of Ovid's *Metamorphoses* tells how King Pygmalion falls in love with a naked ivory statue that he has carved. When he prays to the goddess of love, Aphrodite fulfills his longing: Galatea is brought to life as the mirror image of his desire. Another example: on the eve of his foot race with Atalanta, Hippomen prays to Aphrodite, and she gives him three golden apples. Atalanta sacrifices the race when she stops to pick up Aphrodite's apples, but she wins a husband.

Her trickery, her enticements, ensnare both sexes, but more frequently women are the victims. Perhaps this is because she does not easily tolerate competition from her own sex in the realm of beauty—as Apuleius' story illustrates. Psyche's beauty makes mortals forget Aphrodite. Furious, Aphrodite wants Psyche destroyed. Instead of crushing her as he is commanded, Amor (the Roman equivalent of Eros) takes Psyche to a secluded paradise where he only appears during the night. In retaliation, Aphrodite sets arduous, even perilous trials for Psyche to surmount before she can win acceptance as his mate.

This spirited goddess can also be harsh on males attempting to bypass her. In Euripides' tragedy *Hippolytus*, Aphrodite brings first devastation and then death to Hippolytus because he ignores her in swearing allegiance to Artemis and celibacy. His stepmother, Phaedra, is used by the goddess to avenge this neglect. Phaedra, trapped by her passionate feelings for her stepson, commits suicide. In the play, Aphrodite says: "Those that respect my power I advance to honor, but bring to ruin all who vaunt themselves at me."

Aphrodite not only stirs emotions, she intensifies them, both internally and in feelings toward others. Using the subjective voice of unfulfilled longing that she inspires, Sappho, her devotee, sings of the power of love. Ninety-five percent of Sappho's poetry, largely devoted to Aphrodite's realm, was burned publicly, first by Greek Orthodox fanatics and later by French and German Crusaders in the Fifth Crusade, revealing the harsh depth of emotional reaction that Aphrodite stirs. Friedrich comments on the tragic obliteration: "This compulsion to burn Sappho indicates that her vision threatened the Christian foundations of patriarchy, hypocrisy, and puritanism....Of her five-hundred-odd poems, there survive to this day between six and seven hundred lines. Her work was extirpated from the Greek-speaking world just as ruthlesrly and almost as successfully as the image of her persona, Aphrodite." None are ever neutral toward Aphrodite; many fear falling under her aphroditic sway.

Despite critics like Martin Nilsson who dismiss the goddess of desire as merely a natural instinct, and others who deplore her vanity, her tendency to dawdle, and her hedonism, I am convinced that Aphrodite's sway, then as now, is the *most potent* of the twelve Olympians. Not even Homer's efforts in the *Iliad* to make her a figure of ridicule and to dramatize her ineffectiveness on the battlefield are persuasive. It is mockery aimed at mitigating Aphrodite's terrible power to turn lives upside down and change destinies. Homer allows only the remotest recognition of her might. Yet I believe she emerges as *the* dominant force in the *Iliad*, casting her shadow over the panorama of the Trojan War and its far-flung consequences. Perhaps, in the patriarchy that Homer exalted, it would have been difficult to directly acknowledge the strength of female sexuality that Aphrodite embodied. It was easier to accept multiple acts of lust by males (e.g. Zeus).

Aphrodite's commanding power over events leading to the Trojan War begins with Paris' decision to give her the golden apples, inscribed "to the fairest of them all." Eris, goddess of Discord, had found the perfect way to disturb the world when she brought the apples to the wedding of Thetis, to which she had not been invited. Paris' decision initiates the action that is responsible for Helen leaving a respected position in a noble household with a beloved husband and child to follow Paris to

Troy. Aphrodite's influence is never far from the vortex of action.

In the song of the poet Demedocus in *The Odyssey*, it might seem once again that Aphrodite is being ridiculed. The story relates how Hephaistos traps Aphrodite and Ares with golden chains while they are making love. But even this occasion, which might have ended badly, is turned by Hermes into a cause of merriment when he mentions that he and many others would be happy to take Ares' place, even at the risk of being caught. When released, Aphrodite quickly skips off to Cyprus to be renewed and refreshed and to continue her endeavors. She is simply fulfilling her nature.

Aphrodite bridges the extremes between dynamic opposites. Her great power is this special attribute, a subtle force that can govern the most severe, excruciating tensions, acute and polarized dissociations, often resolving them into new formations. She is the prototype of all archetypes, as she structurally unites extensions and subtleties of dimensions of being that only derive from passion. Karl Kerényi puts it nicely: "[She] makes pale every sort of partialness. She is present when wholeness emerges from the halves and when the resolved opposites become the indissoluble goldenness of life." Christine Downing has this to add: "We may learn from you [Aphrodite] a way of knowing ourselves and the world that comes only through turning in love toward another." Ginette Paris relates her power to bind cultural as well as personal contradictions: "She [Aphrodite] revitalizes the tension between opposites and yet permits union between them: nature and culture, body and spirit, sky and ocean, woman and man."

Friedrich observes another of the contrasting characteristics that make Aphrodite so potent and so dangerous: the combining of sex and sensuousness with maternity and motherliness. Together these qualities bestow on her an intimidating concentration of power intended, as Friedrich puts it, "to threaten the male's image of his authority by bringing into the open the sexual and emotional power of the female." The exposure of this tensile bond reveals the dangers inherent in the incest taboo, perhaps accounting for the blanket repression of Aphrodite's influence in our world.

In our day we find it hard to accept a philosophical precept obvious to the Greeks—that beauty is purposeful to the soul's destiny. Ron Schenk makes a cogent point: "For us to recover the psychological value of beauty, we would need to restore the 'metaphysical dignity' it held for the Greeks."

To single out beauty and call it a grace is a hurdle for many. Even more disturbing is the uneasy connection between beauty, sexual attraction, and the desiring nature that yearns for a connection with the gods. Through studies of Sufi mysticism, Henry Corbin reaffirms that human beauty has sacred meaning. This close alignment infers that a longing for beauty will lead to the knowledge of the radiant individual soul and to the awareness of the reach of our desires. Plato's point. And Frederick Turner's.

On the individual level, we may sometimes intuit that those who attract us sexually offer us an insight into soul-making. In today's psychological parlance we say that our passions for another are projections of our fantasies. We can look favorably on them as reminders that it is possible to stay some of the projection and develop those sought-for, missing qualities of soul in ourselves. The quickening of interest, called an anima or animus response by Jung, is a vital initiation of the individuation process. Transformation of sexual attraction into lasting love only follows when beauty is discovered as an inward as well as an outward grace. Nancy Qualls-Corbett affirms this point: "Aphrodite embodies not just instinct, but also the soul's desire. In a mature alliance, the partners realize both the erotic and the spiritual potential of the relationship."

In the West, commencing with Hesiod and Homer and continuing with Christianity, the realm of Aphrodite has been diminished. Whatever vestiges that might have remained were exorcised by Puritanism in its rejection of sensual pleasure. In the Islamic world today, any woman with aphroditic qualities is considered a seductress, deserving of punishment. The basic schism lies in the insistence of a disjunction between the mind, the body, and the spirit. Rejection of the body, especially the female body, as the temple of the soul/spirit produces a total distaste for any connection between sexual and religious urges. The resulting loss brings terrible splits in the psyche and threatens the nonbeliever with the violence of fundamentalistic fervor.

The mystery and magic of sexuality and spirituality are not so dissimilar, since each draws us out of our exclusivity. The Tantric tradition in India openly accepts the *mysterium tremendum* involved in both realms of being. The connection is obliquely acknowledged in the imagery of the church or nun as bride of Christ and in such expressions as "the passion of Christ." We need to be reminded that the white dove of Aphrodite is also the dove of the Holy Spirit.

The prevailing debasement of Aphrodite's gifts prompts females to dislike their bodies and to suffer perpetual dissatisfaction in trying to live up to some abstract standard of beauty, with little awareness of individual appeal. Women despair about beauty, frantically seeking to take the ugliness out of their bodies, some even resorting to the extreme emaciation of anorexia. Under Aphrodite's aegis, beauty is a state of grace. As early as the fourth century B.C., Aphrodite was beginning to receive short shrift, as the Eros myth superseded the Aphroditic in Plato. Unruly Eros was reintroduced into our time by Freud, more as a concept than as an image. We might ask: why Eros and not Aphrodite? Classically he is the errand boy, but she is the power behind him. If we enlarged the erotic with the aphroditic, modern psychology would be very different. Hillman points out that instead of translating libido as "the visible beauty of soul, it was translated into a Promethean concept of psychic energy."

Eric Fromm contends that Freud's extreme patriarchalism "led him to the assumption that sexuality per se is masculine, and thus made him ignore the specific female sexuality." Fromm's criticism of Freud's theory is "not that he overemphasized sex, but his failure to understand sex deeply enough." Both male and female sexuality is lived out in our time in maladapted ways. Bachelard suggests that we honor both maleness and femaleness and that our goal should be "to live at both poles of our androgynous being."

Jung acknowledges the power of Eros is foundational, contrasting it to Logos, but he does not go far enough in recognizing the manifest aspect of beauty and desire to further Psyche's journey. Again Hillman reminds us that Jung, in separating psychology from aesthetics, failed to appreciate the importance of manifest beauty: "We force Aphrodite to return only via her diseases—transference, sensualism, naturalism, concretism, and the flesh as sheer superficiality."

Perhaps the neglect of Aphrodite stems from what one writer calls "our decadent Puritanism," which robs our culture as well as our personal life of multiplicity. Ginette Paris points out that "real cultural poverty is expressed by the total absence of Aphrodite" and that the "lack of Aphrodite brings frigidity in all interpersonal relationships." Slighting Aphrodite makes us search for beauty in aberrant ways, in pseudo-pleasures, in ever more glossy surroundings, and in rampant materialistic consumption. Is this punishment for demythologizing her glorious gold, allowing it only commercial value, thus limiting us to a rapacious and sterile search for it in a debased form? Celebratory pleasures are undervalued in our time, replaced by weird forms of sensationalism and hedonistic rituals. Is this also her revenge? An empty search for sensual satisfaction, the trivializing of our desires, the working out of them in undercover ways has followed in her vanishing wake.

A culture that spawns rampant pornography or rape as a ritual of manhood provides poor substitutes for the exalted and pure passion that a loving encounter can bring. By confusing the basic human need for beauty, we end up seeking transformation or escape from twentieth century sordidness through drugs. If we cultivated Aphrodite's attributes, the missing elements in our thirsting search for beauty might emerge again. If we made this eclectic goddess more welcome in our midst, we might recapture and honor those images that illumine the constructive aspect of our desires.

SOME NEW ASPECTS OF

HERMES

ROBERT SARDELLO

Afte reading and thinking a great deal about Hermes, I went looking through many books for a work of art, a picture which sums up and manifests the very essence of Hermes. A stroke of luck, a windfall, a happy accident, brought me to the image, the exactly right image with which to begin. Lo and behold, the image which shows most what Hermes is all about can be found in the Dallas Museum of Art! It is this sculpture of the top of a caduceus [illustration page 118]. The caduceus, you know, is the magical wand carried by Hermes, said to have been given to him by Apollo in exchange for the lyre, made from the shell of a tortoise, invented by Hermes on the day of his birth. The modern version of the caduceus is the emblem of the medical profession, which undoubtedly has lost the memory of its origin, and, more tragically, has lost the whole concept of healing with which this instrument is connected.

This image is from the early fifth century B.C. Only the top is preserved, the culmination point of the two snakes entwined around a staff. In many early representations of the caduceus we cannot tell for sure that the wand is related to snakes, but there is no mistake here. Further, we notice that the snakes are bearded. Now, here is what I suggest this image says to us, which is the conclusion of all I have to say about the essence of Hermes. Let me state the conclusion first, and then we shall see what can be said to warrant such a conclusion concerning the nature of this god. I believe this image is a version of something very deep and basic to the Greek imagination, what the Greeks bequeathed to us signifying the task of humanity: "Know Thyself." The bearded snakes evoke that kind of wisdom, to come to the full wisdom of oneself, the capacity to look at ourselves in our full nature. Truly, each of the gods and goddesses can be understood as prompting the quest for self-understanding. What is unique about that task, and what constitutes the central meaning of Hermes, is that "know thyself" means know the true being of your bodily nature in that aspect that is closest to the earth. Through proper intelligence, this can be transformed into knowing that in our bodily being we are also soul and spirit. Face yourself in your bodily nature, for there you will find soul and spirit. There you will confront the continually regenerating soul, you will find the mystery of reincarnation, of the soul winding its way toward its return to the spiritual world, through the agency of the body. Death is not the end of life, its cessation, but, as the snake sheds its skin, so the soul sheds it body periodically to be renewed again in a further life. Life and death are intertwined, not opposed to one another. Further, this image states: "Face thyself in your bodily being in its three-fold nature of spirit, body, and soul in one, and you will know yourself in your divine being; you will gradually come to recognize that your task is to enter into the realm of the gods, not through relinquishing but through transforming your body." Thus, the intelligence that can dissolve the opposites of life and death, the intelligence that can learn to traverse the three–fold world of the spirit, the soul, and the body, led the Egyptians before the Greeks to speak of thrice-greatest Hermes, Hermes Trismegistos, who was said to be an actual human being, the embodiment of the Egyptian deity, Thoth.

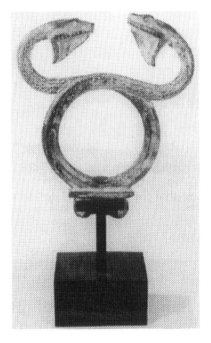

Upper part of Caduceus (Hermes Staff); Bronze. Greece, early 5th Century B.C. Dallas Museum of Art, gift of the Junior League of Dallas.

This wisdom the Greeks inherited, and it was recreated and further developed in them through the mythology of Hermes.

Now that you know where we are going, let's do the work of getting there. The sources for doing so are three-fold; first, the Homeric "Hymn to Hermes"; second, the absolutely marvelous little book entitled *Hermes—Guide of Souls* by Karl Kerényi; and third, the very scholarly but nonetheless exciting book by Jenny Strauss Clay entitled *The Politics of Olympus*.

The determination of the essence of the Greek gods and goddesses belongs to the art of the poet. Without the poet we are faced with fragmented historical conceptions of gods and goddesses that vary according to local regions and cities. Thanks to the poet the countless local cults of Greece are brought into a true image, a permanent configuration assembled in one superterrestrial abode, Olympos. Olympos functions as an imaginal place, a "mundus imaginalis," in the words of Henri Corbin. Through this place all actual places and creatures come into being. The stories of the gods recounted in *The Homeric Hymns* belong to what the great mythologist Mircea Eliade calls "true stories." Eliade says these stories differ from tales and fables which, even though they caused changes in the world, have not altered the human condition, as such. Myths, or true stories, do alter the human condition; the human today is the direct result of those mythical events; we are constituted by those events, because, Eliade says, something happened in *illo tempore*, something that forever changed the fabric of time itself. The Homeric "Hymn to Hermes" is such a true alteration of being human.

Hermes is the son of Zeus and a cave nymph Maia. Maia warrants particular attention. The nymphs are neither human nor divine. They are associated with the very source of life, and thus are found in groves of trees, fresh springs, new plants, wherever life is emerging. Later we shall see that Hermes is very closely related to the mystery of trees, bridging as they do the depths of the earth and even the underworld with the heavens above. Standing more or less mid-way between mortal and immortal, nymphs are the wet nurses of divine children. Maia is such a nurse-mother to Hermes, and is very special.

In one place she is named the daughter of the titan Atlas, and in another place she is said to be the eldest star of the constellation known as the Pleiades. She spans the complete range of being, from the highest to the lowest, and is the bearer of the interchangeability of the highest with the lowest. Hermes serves the full range of the these archetypal dimensions, from the lowest bodily function to the highest, most lofty abode of the gods. The alchemists fully understood their patron, Mercurius, for alchemical work began with dung and ended with dung, which for them was the same as gold. The point is to transform dung into gold, but such transformation entailed seeing through the dung to the gold; when the gods are seen in everything, everything holds a god. But, I suggest, this capacity is due as much to Maia as to Hermes. In the Hymn, his wily cunning and thievery secure not only his place in the pantheon but also that of Maia. At one remarkable point in the Hymn, when Hermes arrives back home after stealing Apollo's cattle, he says to his mother: "I'm ready to do whatever I must so that you and I will never go hungry. You are wrong to insist we live in a place like this...Better always to live in the company of other deathless ones...rich, glamorous, enjoying heaps of grain...than forever to sit by ourselves in a gloomy cave." Now this statement is quite perplexing because we do not find Maia, at the end, among the Olympians, as we do Hermes. Yet, we have nowhere the feeling that he deserts his nurse-mother. We must conclude, I propose, that the actions of Hermes secure not only his immortality, but also prepare the possibility for the immortality of everything earthly, which is ultimately to say, Earth herself. Hermes prepares this possibility through creating hermetic consciousness.

The union of Maia with Zeus takes place in secret, far from Olympos, in the dead of night. But, this affair of Zeus' is distinguished from his infamous amatory pursuits with mortals in that Maia is dignified with the epithet "revered." This is no one-night fling. We detect an equality between Zeus and Maia, which produces a very special son. What most distinguishes the son of this union is that he does not know who he is. Hermes does not know whether he is divine or mortal. He is the last born of the Olympians, born far away from the company of the gods, at night, in a secluded cave. And dad left without telling him anything of his nature. At least, he bears a special relation to Hestia, the first born of the Olympians. Connected with the hearth, Hestia presides over the space and place of Olympos. Within this space all of the gods and goddesses preside over categories of being. But the Olympian world, when completed, forms a static universe outside time. Hermes has two tasks, tasks that he knows only by carrying them out. First, since everything has been allotted on Olympos, there is nothing for him. He must come to his portion by thieving it. In the way that Hermes carries out this thievery and in what follows, the static Olympian world is changed into a dynamic, moving universe; that is to say, this place outside of time, immortal, becomes, through Hermes, intimately linked with the temporal world of mortals. And, in turn, the temporal world of mortals becomes infused with the imagination of the timeless and permanent. Thus, as we shall see, Hermes is the god presiding over borders, making possible commerce between the divine and the human. Further, this commerce suggests that the divine world is affected, changed by what occurs in the human world, that the divine world is not fixed, that what we do alters the divine. Now, one further element is needed to bring the flow between divine and human into circulation. At this point, we have the two-fold Hermes. Keep in mind that Hermes is three-fold, and we will get to that essential third later. I do want to point out here the difference between Hermes and that other notorious thief, Prometheus. Prometheus steals fire from the gods and that theft brings about the establishment of human civilization. But it is a one-way theft, cutting mortals off from the divine world, setting us off on the direction of making a world without an inherent divine element. The Hermetic theft, I suggest, is more fruitful because it provides a direction for the making of a spiritual culture since hermeticism, unlike technology, renews rather than depletes the world.

Let us consider this theft of Hermes as presented in the Homeric Hymn. On the day of his birth Hermes leaves the dark seclusion of the cave of his origin and ventures forth into the day. But we must never forget his origin in Night, for Night is not just a time but a state of consciousness. It is not a state of sleep, for we are also told in many ways of the constant mental agility of Hermes—his restless powers of observation, a glance that swiftly lights on all relevant details and misses nothing of importance, and a lightning-swift intelligence that cuts through all obstacles to reach its goal. Taken together, these two qualities—night consciousness and intelligence—give us a real feeling for hermetic consciousness, which can be best named meditative consciousness or intuition, for that is exactly what happens in the kind of meditation required for the development of the human spirit. In meditation, one relinquishes brain activity, enters into a state of darkness that is nonetheless light and sees things in a flash that are invisible to the senses. At the moment Hermes leaves the cave, at that very transition between Night and Light, he spies a tortoise. Persuasively, seductively, deceptively, he speaks of seeing new possibilities for the tortoise, which he proceeds to kill, and, from the shell, invents the lyre. That is the kind of intelligence I am talking about—not logical, but swift, incredibly creative, sometimes cruel, seeing the possibilities of the moment. Later, this lyre will get Hermes out of a great deal of trouble with Apollo. Not only is a new musical instrument invented, but, as with all things devised by hermetic consciousness, it is not just an addition to what is, but a radical change in consciousness itself. For the lyre provides the possibility, hitherto unknown, of the musician being both the singer and the player at the same time. Apollo will love this offering, because it is a new order of things that does not destroy the old order but expands it from within. Hermes in this respect differs from Dionysos, who brings about change through radical disruption of an order that has become crystallized. Hermes goes then from the cave and finds fifty cattle that belong to Apollo, steals them with great craftiness. He steals the cattle because he feels hunger. Now, only mortals feel hunger, not gods, so at this point, Hermes is unsure of who he is. Hermes kills two of the cattle; quite significant, for since these cattle belong to Apollo, they belong to the realm of the immortal.

Hermes' theft and killing remove cattle from the immortal domain to the mortal world. The remaining forty-eight cattle are transformed into domestic animals who graze on ordinary grass and who increase and multiply; they are removed from the divine sphere, and become a fundamental basis of human commerce. Hermes thus seems mortal; certainly he is on that side. He proceeds to arrange what appears to be a sacrifice to the gods, dividing up the meat into twelve portions to honor the pantheon; notice, however, that he craftily includes himself as the twelfth Olympian. Further, what appears to be a sacrifice is not, for he divides the twelve portions of meat equally. If it were a sacrifice to the gods, each god would be given an unequal share, a portion determined by their particular degree of honor. Thus, Hermes does not prepare a sacrifice, but a feast. Indeed, one of the epithets of Hermes is "companion of the feast." Here we have a feast celebrating equality; that is to say, Hermes alters the hierarchical character of the gods without attempting to destroy it, introducing a new element that says when, through Hermes, the gods are brought close to the realm of the mortals, they are all equal; each has an equal part to play in the realm of becoming. In the timeless realm of being, there is a hierarchy of order. In the temporal order of becoming, all are equal.

Now, when the feast has been prepared, Hermes makes a discovery. He cannot eat the meat. At that moment he realizes himself as a god, for gods do not have hunger and do not eat meat. From that moment in the Hymn we see a remarkable change in Hermes; he is completely confident of himself; he is the god whose territory is not a place but the making of transitions between places; the individual domain of the gods is disrupted without being destroyed; they are brought into relation with each other, an active flow among them now occurs, because he has introduced the order of equality between them. The division between the divine and the mortal realm is bridged, a two-way bridge of commerce and exchange back and forth is brought about by ambiguous Hermes whose nature is to traverse both realms. What is most amazing about Hermes is that his actions accomplish all of this without revolution, without incurring the wrath of the gods.

Zeus, in fact, is delighted with the whole thing.

Apollo is not initially so delighted. Angry at the theft of his cattle, he goes stalking Hermes and takes him before Zeus. Hermes bold-facedly denies the accusations of Apollo, but is reconciled with Apollo only when he gives Apollo the gift of the lyre. First, Hermes sings, and his song is a theogony, a praising of all of the gods, including himself. He then gives Apollo the lyre, a very clever move, for Apollo as the god who maintains order and observes hierarchies and distinctions, especially those separating gods and mortals, Hermes wins over by giving him an instrument that is, at the same time, a new way of order-ing things—one that no longer separates singer and player, but brings them together in exactly the manner that Hermes brings the gods together in a new order of equality—and the way Hermes also brings the gods and mortals into connection through the back and forth of exchange. Now, Apollo is delighted and gives Hermes the caduceus. Zeus is also delighted and gives Hermes the exclusive right to pene-trate into the underworld and to carry souls to Hades. This takes us to the third domain of Hermes; he crosses the boundaries of the god's separation from each other; he bridges the boundary between the divine and the human; and he bridges these two realms with the underworld. Let us now look more deeply into this aspect of three–fold Hermes.

The caduceus given to Hermes by Apollo, and the somewhat questionable gift of becoming guide of souls to the underworld given by Zeus, are the elements we need to transport us to the third aspect of hermetic imagination. This aspect is by far the most difficult to com-prehend, for after all, how could access to the underworld of dead souls be a gift? Besides that, Hecate is already designated as guide of dead souls. The key has already been given when we remember that the territory belonging to Hermes is transition across borders, and it is of the utmost importance that we remember that his transits always go both ways! The caduceus has a two-fold power. It puts souls to sleep, and it awakens them again. Here, then, we are taken into a great mys-tery. Hermes, as Petronius says later in history, "is the one who leads souls away and leads them back again." We confront here the mystery of reincarnation. We have been led to it by necessity, for it is inconceivable that the god who bridges worlds both back and forth would, when it comes to the underworld, suddenly find himself on a one-way street. However, I do not want to arrive at this conclusion through logic but through an exploration of the images themselves.

The image confirming that indeed the great gift of Hermes' access to the underworld, that the very essence of the gift concerns guiding them back as well, is the much misunderstood and maligned image of the herm. The word "herm" means "stone heap," and also refers to a particular phallic image of Hermes placed along the road as a guide for travelers, and also at the borders of particular precincts. The herm is a peculiar image, which except for the erect phallus and the head, remains featureless. One additional aspect of the herm, however, is of great importance, as we shall see. It rests on a square base. I must depart from the Homeric Hymn to consider the herm, because there is, exactly at the point we are now considering, a break in the text, a lost fragment. This gap is filled by the research of Karl Kerényi.

Our question is simply this: how do souls return from the underworld? And our answer is this image. The reincarnation of souls takes place through the phallus. Hermes is not to be confused with gods associated with sexuality or with love. The intent of this image is not sexual or erotic. Further, and this is, I know, difficult, but it must be said, this image of the phallic herm is as much feminine as it is masculine; nay, even more strongly put, the essence of this image is feminine insofar as what is depicted here is Hermes emerging from the very source of life; Hermes is an expression of this source of life, which is feminine. It may be more clear if I say it this way: Hermes is in service to the great goddess, the source of life. Forgive me if I say it very directly: the phallus is merely the conduit through which the seed, which belongs to the goddess Demeter-Persephone, is transported into the earthly world.

The herm is characterized, first, by the four-sided base. The figure does not so much rest on top of this base as it emerges from the base, coming up from the earth and from the underworld. The quadratic form, which the image emphasizes by repeating it at the place of the arm of the figure, is an archetypal expression of totality, rooted in the very foundation of the world. Of great interest is the fact that the herm, a border marker, does not express the sculptured form of a man. Only three elements are present—the quadratic base, the phallus, and the head. We must read the image moving from below, as if he is exuded from the earth. The phallus, in this case, partakes of this movement from below, the extension of the below in the horizontal direction, moving souls back out into the world, shamelessly—the transition from the underworld to the earthly. And, in keeping with this movement, the head too must be seen as the culmination of the movement from below, indicating that it is through the meditative intelligence, rooted in the soul world, that the reincarnated soul penetrates into the heavenly sphere. Thus, the image of the herm carries out in a reverse, mirror-image the transitions, the boundary crossing that we have seen in the other direction—as above so below, so say the alchemists, whose central secret was Mercurius, that is to say, thrice-greatest Hermes.

HERMES

This reading of the image of the herm is verified through the presence of the small tree standing behind the herm. Rooted in the ground, deriving its very source of life from the roots which extend as deep as the underworld, the tree extends its branches into the world and reaches toward the heavens. And, as the tree grows, it is pervaded, not only by the forces of life, but also with the forces of death. The tree grows only because part of it also dies. Perhaps that is why, in the image, we are to contemplate the trunk and the branches rather than a tree in full leaf. Only as the trunk dies into the bark do the branches grow, and, only as the branches die do they extend themselves. At the same time, only as the outer covering dies, does the sap of life course through the tree. This intertwining of life and death dissolves death as opposite to life, a dissolution belonging to the essence of Hermes. Further, we find, when we look at a tree, that its movement is not straightforward but proceeds by branching in many directions, all headed in the same general direction. Thus, Hermes is the guide of the traveler, the journeyer; we see him as such in the journey of the *Odyssey*. The journey concerns the movement of the soul in life, which never proceeds in linear fashion, and involves many deaths within the course of life.

Ancient mythology of Hermes presents a picture of modern hermetic consciousness. This consciousness consists of the capacity of "seeing through." The invisible flow of back and forth connections, relating one thing to another, is seen through the visible diversity of phenomena making a kinship among all beings. This mode of consciousness is not a natural gift but must be earned through experience, through the discipline of creating connections between opposites, vertical correspondences between the above and the below, and horizontal correspondences between the past and the future. The former is called symbolic imagination and the latter mythological imagination. The point at which these two cross constitutes the hermetic moment of intuition. The practice of intuition requires the development of the ability to concentrate without effort. Just as the magician or juggler has had to train and work for a long time before attaining the ability to concentrate without effort, and much experience is required. So too, those who make use of intuition have acquired experience through study and teaching. At the same time, the work of the hermeticist is always play. The hermetic vision of the unity between things and beings, through the immediate, swift perception of their correspondences is analogous to the attitude of the child. Thus, Hermes constantly appears both as child and as old man, at work, acquiring experience, always in an attitude of play, always seeing unrelated things as related. The hermeticist makes, through taking or thieving, what the world has to offer and by twisting it into new forms, a synthesis between creative spontaneity, or the unconscious, and deliberately executed activity, or consciousness. It is the state of consciousness Jung calls "individuation." This presentation, I sincerely, but not too sincerely, hope, has itself been an exercise and illustration of hermetic consciousness. The proper execution of this mode of activity creates magic, the continual intertwining of the divine and the mortal, each powerfully affecting the other. To speak of proper execution implies that hermeticism can also be carried out improperly. That is to say, there is Play and there is play. Anyone who confuses concentration without effort with streams of simple associations is not a magician but a charlatan. The distinction may be clear, but I must end in true hermetic fashion. Only by following this path yourself will you determine, by actual engagement in the activity, how much of what has been said is magic and how much is charlatanism.

SELECTED BIBLIOGRAPHY

Atwood, Margaret. *Selected Poems 1965–1975*. Boston: Houghton
    Mifflin, 1976.

Atwood, Margaret. *Survival: A Thematic Guide to Canadian Literature*.
    Toronto: Anansi, 1972.

Berry, Patricia. "Neurosis and the Rape of Demeter/Persephone,"
    Echo's Subtle Body. Dallas: Spring Publications, 1987.

Bolen, Jean Shinboda. *Goddess in Everywoman*. New York: Harper &
    Row, 1984.

Burkert, Walter. *Greek Religion*. Trans. John Raffan. Cambridge, Mass.:
    Harvard Univ. Press, 1985.

Clay, Jenny Strauss. *The Politics of Olympus: Form and Meaning in The
    Major Homeric Hymns*. Princeton: Princeton Univ. Press, 1989.

Collignon, Maxime. *Manual of Mythology in Relation to Greek Art*.
    Trans. Jane E. Harrison. New York: Caratzas Brothers, 1982.

Downing, Christine. *The Goddess: Mythological Images of the Feminine*.
    New York: Crossroad Publishing Co., 1981.

Euripides. *Hippolytus*. Trans. David Grene. In *Greek Tragedies*. Ed.
    David Grene and Richmond Lattimore. Second Edition.
    Volume 1. Chicago: Univ. Chicago Press, 1991. 233–95.

Farnell, Lewis Richard. *The Cults of the Greek States*. Volume 2.
    1896–1905. 5 volumes. New Rochelle, NY: Caratzas Brothers,
    1977.

Friedrich, Paul. *The Meaning of Aphrodite*. Chicago: Univ. Chicago
    Press, 1978.

Gordon, Caroline. *The Glory of Hera*. Garden City, NY: Doubleday, 1972.

Griffin, Susan. *Woman and Nature: The Roaring Inside Her*. New York:
    Harper and Row (Colophon Books), 1980.

Harding, M. Esther. *Woman's Mysteries: Ancient and Modern*. New
    York: G.P. Putnam's Sons, 1971.

Hesiod. *The Works and Days, Theogony, The Shield of Herakles*. Trans. Richmond Lattimore. Michigan: Univ. Michigan Press, 1968.

Hillman, James. *The Dream and the Underworld*. New York: Harper and Row, 1979.

Homer. *The Iliad*. Trans. Robert Fagles. New York: Penguin Books, 1991.

Homer. *The Odyssey*. Trans. Richmond Lattimore. New York: Harper & Row, 1967.

Homer. *The Homeric Hymns*. Trans. Apostolos N. Athanassakis. Baltimore: Johns Hopkins Univ. Press, 1976.

Homer. *The Homeric Hymns*. Trans. Charles Boer. University of Dallas, Irving, TX: Spring Publications, 1979.

Jung, C.W. and Kerényi, Karl. *Essays on a Science of Mythology*. Trans. R.F.C. Hull. New Jersey: Princeton Univ. Press, 1971.

Kerényi, Karl. *Goddesses of Sun and Moon*. Dallas: Spring Publications, 1979.

Kerényi, Karl. *Hermes–Guide of Souls*. Trans. Murray Stein. Zurich: Spring Publications, 1976.

Kerényi, Karl. *Zeus and Hera Archetypal Image of Father, Husband, and Wife*. Trans. Christopher Holme. New Jersey: Princeton Univ. Press, 1975.

Nilsson, Martin. *Greek Piety*. Trans. Herbert Jennings Rose. New York: W.W. Norton & Company, 1969.

Otto, Walter F. *The Homeric Gods–The Spiritual Significance of Greek Religion*. New York: Pantheon Books, 1954.

Ovid, *Metamorphoses*. Trans. Mary M. Innes. New York: Penguin Books, 1978.

Paris, Ginette. *Pagan Meditations*. Dallas: Spring Publications, 1986.

Pindar. *Odes*. Ed. and trans. by Cecil Maurice Bowra. Oxford Classical Texts, 2nd edition. Oxford: Oxford University Press, 1947.

Sappho: Lyrics in the Original Greek with Translations by Willis Barnstone. Garden City, NY: Anchor Books, Doubleday & Co., 1965.

Schenk, Ronald. *The Soul of Beauty*. London and Toronto: Associated University Presses, 1992.

Sculley, Vincent. *The Earth, the Temple, and the Gods: Greek Sacred Architecture*. Second Edition. New Haven and London: Yale Univ. Press, 1979.

Warner, Marina. *Monuments & Maidens–The Allegory of the Female Form*. New York: Atheneum, 1985.

Welty, Eudora. "Moon Lake." In *The Collected Stories of Eudora Welty*. New York: Harcourt Brace Jovanovich, 1980.

Contributors

WILLIAM BURFORD, PH.D.
> Poet

DONALD COWAN, PH.D.
> Physicist; University Professor, University of Dallas

LOUISE COWAN, PH.D.
> Literary critic; University Professor, University of Dallas

DONA S. GOWER, PH.D.
> Director of the Dallas Institute's Teachers Academy

EILEEN GREGORY, PH.D.
> Chairman, Department of English, University of Dallas

LYLE NOVINSKI
> Artist; Chairman, Department of Art, University of Dallas

DANIEL RUSS, PH.D.
> Headmaster, Trinity Christian Academy

ROBERT SARDELLO, PH.D.
> Co-Founder of the School of Spiritual Psychology

JOANNE H. STROUD, PH.D.
> Author; Director, Dallas Institute Publications

GAIL THOMAS, PH.D.
> Cultural Critic; Director of the Dallas Institute

FREDERICK TURNER, PH.D.
> Poet, Founders Professor of Arts and Humanities,
> University of Texas at Dallas

MARY VERNON
> Artist; Chair, Studio Arts Division, Meadows School
> of the Arts, Southern Methodist University